black crusader Frederick Douglass

black crusader Frederick Douglass

by Corinne K. Hoexter

illustrated with photographs and prints

RAND McNALLY & COMPANY   Chicago New York San Francisco

B
Douglass

for Rolf

H P

contents

acknowledgments

When I first became interested in the life of Frederick Douglass, I used to question my friends to see if they knew who he was. Most had never heard of him or confused him with Stephen Douglas, Lincoln's opponent in the famous 1858 debates.

The more I read Frederick Douglass's speeches and writings, the more they had a haunting familiarity. Didn't echoes of his ideas, and even his words, appear daily in the newspapers as the fever chart of the civil rights movement of our own times was being recorded? The hopes and struggles and short-lived triumphs of the early sixties, the doubts of the middle sixties, and the disillusionments and dark prophecies of the late sixties were all experienced by Douglass or foreshadowed by his predictions.

It seemed to me that today's young activists, living in the heat of the conflict generated by our great unsolved "American dilemma," might find an illumination of the roots of that conflict in the story of Frederick Douglass.

My quest for Douglass, as he was seen and known by his family, friends, and contemporaries, was immeasurably aided by the formidable resources and immensely knowledgeable and helpful staff of the research libraries of the New York Public Library.

My special gratitude goes to Miss Elizabeth Roth of the Print Room, who served as my discriminating guide in the world of nineteenth-century prints. The staffs of the Central Reading Room, the American History Room, the Microfilm Room, the Schomburg Collection, the Rare Book Room, the Local History and Genealogy Room, and the Annex, with its collections of early periodicals, all contributed greatly to the success of my search.

Especially exciting and in many ways the high point of my research was my stay in Washington; there Edmund Fitzgerald, Historian; Foster Freeman, Chief of Interpretation; and Mrs. Carol J. Smith, Information Officer—all with the National Park Service, National Capital Parks—East Region—gave me their courteous assistance in using the priceless files of Douglass's letters, speeches, papers, documents, photographs, clippings, and memorabilia of which they are guardians as trustees of the Douglass Memorial Home, Cedar Hill, in Anacostia, Washington, D.C. Moreover, to Edmund Fitzgerald goes special thanks, first of all for showing me Cedar Hill in its present state (where I met and enjoyed the invaluable reminiscences of Mrs. Gladys Parham, long-time caretaker of the home), also for a tour and informal history of Anacostia and Douglass's residence there, and finally for a fascinating afternoon in an old warehouse; examining and discussing the furnishings of Cedar Hill, which are to be refurbished and returned to the home when money becomes available for its restoration. Perhaps more than any of my other research, my conversation—among the desks, hat racks, overstuffed chairs and sofas, books, and portraits—with Mr. Fitzgerald and his able assistant, James Brown, gave me a unique and intimate glimpse of Douglass, the man, in his days as an elder statesman.

I also found my knowledge enriched by my visits to the library and photograph collection of the New York Historical Society. I received insight and aid on two important periods of Douglass's life from the Rochester and Maryland historical societies. Miss Ann Kuss of the New York Central Systems Information Office provided me with some invaluable facts about early New York State railroads.

Finally, I enjoyed a number of hours of concentrated work and found several useful old books in the beautiful reference section of the new Englewood, New Jersey, Public Library.

The illustrations are reprinted with the permission of the following institutions: New York Historical Society, pages 16, 128, 146, 172, 181; the Phelps Stokes Collection of the New York Public Library, pages 38, 60, 110; Penn Central Railroad, page 67; National Capital Region, National Park Service, U.S. Department of the Interior for the Douglass family photographs on pages 169, 191, 197, 200, 208, and the jacket; Rochester Historical Society, page 212. All other pictures are courtesy of the New York Public Library.

photographs and prints

1 **voice of the fugitive**

I will be as harsh as truth, and as uncompromising as justice. On this subject, I do not wish to think, or speak, or write, with moderation.

William Lloyd Garrison, First issue of *The Liberator*

Tempers were rising on the lower deck of the steamer *Telegraph*, but Capt. Lot Phinney stood his ground. He folded his arms and set his jaw so that the bones stood out under his skin.

Confronting him was a group of some forty abolitionists bound for an anti-slavery convention at Nantucket. Their faces looked flushed but earnest, although two of the Negroes in their group had already started to walk back down the gangplank. But the other members of the party, black and white, drew closer to the captain. Murmurs of "outrage" and "disgrace" were heard. Still there was no shaking of fists or raising of voices.

"I'm sorry, ladies and gentlemen," said Captain Phinney in a gruff but level voice. "Those are company rules. I don't make them. No man or woman—of color—may travel in the cabin. We will be glad to accommodate them on deck. It's a fine day. I assure you they'll be comfortable."

August 10, 1841, was indeed a fine morning in New Bedford, Massachusetts. A brisk salt breeze blew in from Buzzards Bay, and the *Telegraph* strained at her moorings.

A thin, balding man in his thirties walked forward. His features were fine, even delicate, but his eyes had an unexpected, piercing clarity which reflected a latent power within. "Captain Phinney," said William Lloyd Garrison in his solemn voice, "are not our colored brethren as respectable in every way as we ourselves? They have paid their full fare and are entitled to their passage."

"I'm sorry, sir," said Captain Phinney, still more gruffly. "I have my orders from the company directors themselves. I will gladly refund anyone's money and set him ashore if he does not like his accommodations. But I swear I shall not start this boat while these—colored—gentlemen remain in the cabin and on the lower deck.

Garrison's voice rose higher, in tones thrilling to those who agreed with him and grating to those who did not. He seemed to speak now not so much for the benefit of his immediate listeners as for some unseen audience inside himself. "See how the long arm of the Slave Power reaches even into the free air of the North, corrupting the hearts of men. None of us shall leave the boat until our colored brothers are properly accommodated."

The abolitionists standing around Garrison and the captain did not clap. But every man and woman seemed to catch some of the sparks given off by his fiery words. One young Negro, who had been looking shyly at the ground, straightened his shoulders and stared directly into the captain's face.

In the face of Garrison's stirring appeal and the growing militancy of the crowd, Phinney dropped back for the first time. His voice was subdued as he suggested that perhaps a solution could be found. Would all the convention delegates be willing to travel on the upper deck if he set it aside for their private use?

Garrison, John A. Collins, Francis Jackson, and some of the other abolitionist leaders walked away from the crowd to consider the suggestion.

The young man who had been so stirred by Garrison's words before could not seem to get enough of looking at the famous abolitionist editor. So busy was Frederick Douglass watching Garrison that he did not notice the attention he

William Lloyd Garrison, aged 35

attracted by his own striking appearance. He was over six feet tall, with a great mane of black curly hair, lips so delicately drawn that they almost formed a Cupid's bow, and brown eyes alive with excitement yet still bearing some memory of past suffering. Probably his most striking feature, especially in profile, was the strong, straight nose that inhaled with the disdain of a thoroughbred.

Perhaps Douglass was recalling Garrison's speech at the annual meeting of the Bristol Anti-Slavery Society the day before. For him it was the exciting culmination of two years of hero worship.

Garrison believed in "moral suasion" and nonresistance,

"complete submission to insults and injuries. . . . " Yet if his manner was calm and serene, his words, which had aroused violence in the North and fury in the South, were not.

One of Garrison's "chief heresies" was that "Prejudice against color was rebellion against God. Of all men beneath the sky, the slaves, because most neglected and despised, were nearest and dearest to his great heart." Garrison therefore said that ministers who defended slavery were "of their father the devil." Churches which embraced slaveholders were "synagogues of Satan." And the Constitution, which permitted slavery, was a "covenant with death and an agreement with hell."

These words were thrilling to a fugitive slave, who still heard a threat in any knock on the door, who feared it might mean a return to the bondage from which he had fled.

Fortunately, the conferring leaders soon came back to announce that a compromise had been reached. The whole party of forty-one abolitionists, of whatever color, should travel on the upper deck. As they filed up the stairs, the rest of the passengers began to follow them because of the intense interest aroused by their confrontation with the captain.

So began Frederick Douglass's first vacation in three years of freedom. The paddle wheels of the *Telegraph* were revolving, slowly at first, then faster and faster. The New Bedford dock grew smaller and then vanished when the boat rounded the point into the open waters of Buzzards Bay and headed east.

The captain, who probably did not want to arouse his unwelcome passengers to further demonstrations, gave permission for an anti-slavery meeting on deck. The Garrisonian abolitionists were always resourceful in turning a seeming setback into a means of advancing their cause. In fact, they thrived on opposition which supplied the publicity they needed.

Francis Jackson, president of the Massachusetts Anti-Slavery Society, was quickly elected to preside over the meeting. Several of the Garrisonian stalwarts, such as Parker Pillsbury,

James Buffum, and John A. Collins, spoke. But the main attention of the party was focused on a very genteel-looking quartet of spectators. It consisted of a gentleman rumored to be a large slaveholder in New Orleans, two elegant ladies, and an Episcopal minister, Dr. Robbins.

The Reverend Dr. Robbins, a mild-looking, white-haired old man, very formal in speech and manners, accepted the invitation of Mr. Jackson to answer the arguments of the abolitionists. The young Frederick Douglass listened to the whole discussion with deep interest. However, the disdainful tightening of his nostrils seemed to grow on hearing Dr. Robbins.

The good doctor assured his listeners that no black man in Africa was so well off as the three million slaves in the South of the United States. "These, he asserted, were well fed and well clothed, *with honorable enjoyment and comfortable homes!*" an anti-slavery newspaper reported with irony. Dr. Robbins personally regretted slavery but did not consider it a sin.

George Bradburn, one of the wittiest of the abolitionists, immediately took the floor. Point by point, he coolly refuted Dr. Robbins's arguments, dwelling especially on the biblical injunction to "love thy neighbor."

As the *Telegraph* docked in Nantucket harbor, the passengers began to spread the story of the meeting on deck and the clash with the captain. The abolitionists' best hopes had been fulfilled. The "needed excitement" had been produced among the inhabitants of Nantucket Island. On this occasion the excitement did not result in the throwing of sticks, stones, and rotten eggs as it often did when abolitionists spoke.

On the morning of August 12, the last day of the convention, Douglass sat on one of the benches, crowded with delegates, in Atheneum Hall. For two days he had listened to stirring denunciations of slavery and voted on resolutions calling for immediate and unconditional emancipation of all slaves in the South.

Most runaway slaves were tracked down, often with dogs, and recaptured or killed, like the unlucky slave at bay in this old woodcut.

The abolitionist who was speaking this morning remarked that there was a temperance convention going on in Nantucket at that very moment. "As they hope for a reformed drunkard to testify for their glorious cause, so we hope for a reformed slaveholder or powerful slave to testify for ours."

The speaker paused and looked around, as if he expected such a person to be mysteriously produced like a rabbit from a hat. A hush fell over the crowd of five hundred. Douglass

looked about to see who might come forward. As he did, he noticed William Coffin, a prominent white abolitionist from New Bedford, coming toward him. Mr. Coffin seemed to think that he had found the man to speak of what it was like to be a slave. He urged Douglass to follow him to the platform.

Douglass usually spoke with some assurance to the bi-weekly meetings of the black abolitionists in New Bedford. In fact, Mr. Coffin remembered hearing him there. Torn between what seemed a duty and his natural diffidence at the thought of addressing such a distinguished audience, Douglass walked slowly after Coffin.

"We have one among us," began Mr. Coffin, "only recently escaped from the house of bondage. I have heard his story, and I assure you it will bear stronger witness to the righteousness of our cause than any words of mine. I present Mr. Frederick Douglass, delegate of New Bedford, but late a graduate of the 'peculiar institution,' who will tell us of his life as a slave in the South."

When he heard these words, Frederick Douglass trembled in every limb. He feared his legs would not support him. He was sure he could not "articulate two words without hesitation and stammering. . . . I am not sure that embarrassment was not the most effective part of my speech, if speech it could be called." So wrote Douglass forty years after this maiden address.

But the audience did not agree with Douglass's low estimate of his ability. As he unfolded the story of his life as a slave, simply but with deep feeling, the crowd was moved to cheers.

From the haze of memory he evoked for them all the places he had known—his grandmother's rough cabin, the great plantation of Colonel Lloyd, the streets and shipyards of Baltimore, the farm of the slavebreaker Covey, and then at last New York following his escape. He recalled fleeting moments or hours of happiness and long months of sorrow and despair; he spoke of the few kind words that had warmed the general coldness and softened the actual brutality.

As he spoke, Douglass gained confidence. He trembled and stuttered no more. His deep, musical voice began to fall into its natural tone and rhythm. He dared not tell them any actual names or places or the manner of his escape. But his descriptions were so graphic and his experiences so moving that many eyes were wet. As a newspaper reporter expressed it:

> Flinty hearts were pierced, and cold ones melted by his eloquence. Our best pleaders for the slave held their breath for fear of interrupting him.

He ended by telling them of his emotions on at last reaching free soil. "It was a moment of the highest excitement I ever experienced. . . . I felt like one who had escaped a den of hungry lions." As Douglass started to leave the platform, a prolonged shout burst from the audience.

Garrison rose to say that

> Patrick Henry, of revolutionary fame, never made a speech more eloquent in the cause of liberty, than the one we [have] just listened to from the lips of [this] hunted fugitive.

The stir created by Douglass's talk did not end with the morning. In the evening he was called upon to speak again and did so, this time with a growing assurance. Though it was near ten o'clock when he had finished speaking, his hearers burst forth with such applause that it seemed they would never let him go.

Seizing the moment of greatest excitement, William Lloyd Garrison rose and gave one of his most eloquent speeches.

> My friends, never have I hated slavery so intensely as at this moment; never before have I perceived the enormous outrage which is inflicted by it on the godlike nature of its victims.
>
> Just now one stood here, in physical proportions and stature commanding and exact—in intellect richly endowed—in natural eloquence a prodigy—in soul manifestly "created but a little lower than the angels"—yet a slave, ay, a fugitive slave—trembling for his safety, hardly daring to believe that on the American soil, a single white person could be found who would befriend him at all hazards, for the love of God and humanity!

Garrison then went on to denounce the Fugitive Slave Law, which compelled the free states to return fugitives like Douglass to their cruel masters.

Even in the Bunker Hill Monument would this poor flying slave be safe from the officers sent to seize him? Perish such a mocking monument to liberty! Where could this man find safety in these boasted Free States? I appeal to your generous hearts!

"Have we been listening to a piece of property, a beast of burden, a chattel personal, or a man?"

"A man! A man!" answered back the five hundred.

"Shall we ever allow him to be carried back into slavery—law or no law, Constitution or no Constitution?"

"NO! NO!" thundered the audience.

"Will you succor and protect him as a brother man—a resident of the old Bay State?" continued Garrison.

"YES!" came a shout that shook the walls.

That heartening assent, commented the *Anti-Slavery Standard*, was worth years of common life.

The abolitionist movement was but one wave of the mighty tide of belief in human liberty and the unique importance of each human soul which had spread to America from Europe in the early 1800s. Out of this basic belief sprang such movements as prison reform, universal suffrage, the rights of workingmen, women's rights, and universal education, as well as abolition.

By 1840 some of the first enthusiasm for abolition had diminished. Also, the South had become more active in stressing through books and pamphlets that the slaves were really happy and well treated.

Thus, when Garrison and other leading abolitionists heard Douglass speak, they realized that he was just the man they had been looking for. Here at last was the truth about slavery, told in inspired language by a slave. Here was a man, intelligent, sensitive, whose tales of brutality in the enlightened slave state of Maryland were attested to by the indelible scars of the lash on his own back. If Douglass could so move the audiences on Nantucket, could he not stir other audiences in the North?

Before the return to New Bedford, John A. Collins, general agent of the Massachusetts Anti-Slavery Society, spoke to Douglass and asked him to become one of their traveling agents. Because of his youth and lack of education, Douglass hesitated. He was afraid they might be disappointed in him. He was a man who all his life, of necessity, had worked with his hands, not with his mind and his tongue.

No, Collins insisted, we need you now, and your people need you now. If he was doubtful, couldn't he try it for just three months? He would be paid $450 a year. The good ladies of New Bedford would see that his wife and children had enough to eat. If Douglass or the society were not satisfied with his accomplishments at the end of the period, they could part friends. He could go back to New Bedford as a laborer. They would send him on the road with an experienced agent like Collins himself, who would help him get started.

Douglass decided to take the risk. For three months he would tell his story to audiences in New England. He would try to explain to them what it meant to be a slave, beginning at the very moment of his birth.

2 plantation ways

. . . there was a saying in Talbot County that God Almighty never intended any white man should own a thousand [slaves], but Colonel Lloyd had 999.

Hulbert Footner, *Rivers of the Eastern Shore*

East of Baltimore, Maryland, and isolated from it by the broad expanse of Chesapeake Bay, lies the flat, sandy peninsula called the Eastern Shore of Maryland. Through this "drowned land" of sand, silt, and clay, many little rivers and streams creep and curl back on themselves till they barely seem to flow. The jagged coastline conceals countless harbors and inlets where yachtsmen and fishermen may anchor for the night.

The air is as softly lazy as the rivers, except in the damp, chill winters. But even then the land is spared the icy blasts of the North. Living here is easy; graciousness, second nature. The rivers, the bay, and the ocean teem with life—crabs, oysters, tuna, bonito, diamond-backed terrapin. Game abounds in the scrubby forests. Vegetables and melons produce several crops a year.

Small wonder that the Eastern Shore is famous for its hospitality and its cooking. The great houses always overflow with company. The poorer people—small fishermen and farmers—always have a piece of fish, some oysters, or a wild duck to offer a guest. It was much the same in the early nineteenth century. No one worked very hard—except the slaves.

Early one June morning in 1824(?), a little slave boy of about seven awoke in his old master's kitchen to the clang and clatter of pots. A rough hand shook him and told him to take his "lazy bones" out from underfoot. It was Aunt Katy, the cook. The boy retreated to a corner. He didn't want to leave the kitchen, where the smell of breakfast hung so deliciously in the air. He felt quite hollow inside, for he had eaten no supper.

Suddenly Aunt Katy lifted a heavy iron kettle of corn-meal mush from a hook over the fireplace. She poured it into a long, low wooden trough and carried it outside, where she set it down on the ground. "Coo-ee, coo-ee," she shouted as if she were calling pigs.

At this signal there was a great rushing and tumbling, not of pigs, but of children, from every corner of the yard. Frederick, the new boy, stood paralyzed with astonishment. His own brother and sisters, whom he had met just the day before, streaked by him as if he weren't there.

As soon as she had elbowed aside the children at the center of the trough to make room for her own brood, Aunt Katy walked back into the kitchen. The children dived for the trough until their chins almost touched the mush. They shoveled it into their mouths with oyster shells, shingles, or, failing those, their hands. By the time Frederick had realized what was happening and had slipped into place beside his brother, Perry, there were only a few bites left. Aunt Katy, returning to pick up the trough, pushed him aside saying it served him right; he'd soon mend his lazy ways. For all his seven years till now, Frederick Augustus Washington Baïley had lived in the warm, loving shelter of Grandmama Betsy's cabin in Tuckahoe, about twelve miles from Easton, Maryland. Like all Old Master's slave women, his mother, Harriet Bailey, had been ordered back to work soon after the birth of her child. His father he had never known. But folks who had seen Frederick's brown cheek nestled against his mother's near-black one whispered that his father had been a white man.

Grandmama Betsy had a "growing hand," a magic touch with all living things. The nets she mended caught the biggest, juiciest fish. The sweet potatoes she planted for all the local

farmers yielded the richest harvest. It was the same with countless children she had raised for her daughters. As little Freddy
grew, his spirit warmed in her affection; his mind took spark
from her shrewd country wisdom.

Yet Grandmama Betsy had deserted him, as she had had
to desert all her other children and grandchildren. For they
belonged to that dread Old Master whom he was soon to meet.

Yesterday Grandmama Betsy had walked with him the
twelve miles from Tuckahoe. Then she had left him, without
even saying good-bye, to sob himself to sleep in the smoky, dirt-
floored kitchen. "This," he wrote years later, "was my first
introduction to the realities of the slave system."

Aunt Katy, the tyrant in Old Master's kitchen, became
Frederick's first trial in his new life. Old Master, who admired
her hardworking ways and her skill in cooking, gave her complete control over the slave children. It was she who received
their monthly allowance of meal to divide among them as she
saw fit. She took an instant dislike to Frederick, so he got even
less than his share of the never-quite-sufficient mush which
was their only food.

If the other children told her "Freddy pushed me" or
"Freddy took my share," it meant no supper for him and perhaps a whipping as well. The gnawing hunger never left him
that first summer. Soon he took to following Aunt Esther, the
kitchen maid, when she shook out the tablecloth, and fighting
for his share of crumbs and small bones with Nep, the dog.

One day, for some small forgotten fault, Aunt Katy told
Frederick he should go all day without food. With that inborn
dignity, which already marked him off from the others and perhaps aggravated Aunt Katy's dislike, he tried not to break down
and cry or beg for a crumb.

Evening came, and Aunt Katy seized a bread knife.
Fiercely she chopped off slices of a large coarse loaf for the
other children and announced she would starve the life out of
Frederick. The sight of them all smugly chewing their bread,

combined with this terrible threat, finally cracked the shell of Frederick's composure. Still he managed to get out of the kitchen before he broke down.

At last he crept wearily back into his corner, too hungry to sleep. As he stared gloomily into the fire he wondered, Why am I treated so? Why must some go hungry while others are so well fed? Luckily he caught sight of a forgotten ear of corn on an upper shelf. He seized it, stripped off as many kernels as his hand could grasp, and sneaked up to the fire to bury them under the ashes.

Still under his lucky star, he piled the toasted kernels on a stool. Never had Grandmama's sweet potatoes tasted more delicious. He hardly noticed the long shadow that bent over him until he was encircled by the warm embrace of his mother. As on those other rare, precious evenings when she could get permission from the overseer, she had walked twelve miles from the farm to see him. She had to be back before dawn on pain of a flogging.

The deep sadness that always lurked under the quiet dignity of her features changed for a moment to joy as she hugged her son to her. To the question of why he was nibbling those bits of corn, he blurted out, "Aunt Katy said she would starve the life out of me."

"Oh, she did, did she," answered his mother, looking at him with intense pity.

Then his mother swept away the hard kernels and put a large ginger cake in his hand. Wrote Frederick later:

> That night I learned as I had never learned before, that I was not only a child but *somebody's* child. I was grander upon my mother's knee than a king upon his throne.

After he had eaten his cake, his mother hovered over him while he drifted off to sleep, sweetly for once. When he awoke

Slave children play in front of a farmhouse and a row of slave cabins, a scene recalling life at Old Master's. (Woodcut by Anderson)

she was gone. Aunt Katy was Aunt Katy still, and no less cruel.

Not long after, he was told his mother had died. For her, perhaps, death was a welcome release; for him it was a perpetual ache. Always he regretted that he had known her so little. Always he was to carry at the back of his mind the image of a woman "tall and finely proportioned, of dark, glossy complexion, with regular features, and amongst the slaves . . . remarkably sedate and dignified."

Fortunately, after sleepy Tuckahoe, Frederick's new home was full of diversion and excitement. The Lloyd plantation, between the Miles and the Wye rivers, was a small kingdom where all the food was raised, all the clothing made, and all the tools and implements and much of the furniture manufactured on the grounds by slave artisans.

Colonel Edward Lloyd, a former governor of Maryland, was the fifth Edward to head his historic family, which had settled in Maryland in 1649. Frederick's master, Captain Aaron Anthony, was Colonel Lloyd's chief agent and steward.

Captain Anthony himself owned two or three farms and twenty or thirty slaves. But Colonel Lloyd owned thirty farms and hundreds of slaves. He had become the biggest cattle raiser and wheat grower in Maryland at a time when large plantations were becoming unprofitable in that state.

Captain Anthony lived with his sons Richard and Andrew, his daughter Lucretia, and Lucretia's husband, Captain Thomas Auld, who commanded the colonel's trading sloop, the *Sally Lloyd*. Captain Anthony, a high-strung man, usually wore a harried frown. Sometimes he would unbend and stroll along the lane, leaning on Frederick's arm, calling him his "little Indian boy." More often he noticed Frederick about as much as if he were a prize bull calf.

Apart from hunger and the venom of Aunt Katy, cold was Frederick's chief enemy in his new life. Like all the slave children, he was given two tow linen shirts a year—no shoes and socks, no trousers, no jackets, and no blanket. If the shirts wore out, he went naked till next allowance day. On cold winter nights he slept in a closet adjoining the kitchen, his head and body in a feed bag, his feet sticking out. His feet were often so frostbitten that "the pen with which I am writing might be laid in the gashes."

However, Frederick's duties were light. He had only to keep the front yard clean, feed the chickens, drive home the cattle, and run errands for Mrs. Lucretia. There was plenty of time left to explore the plantation after he finished his chores.

He might watch the slave artisans in their shops, sweep out the stables to be near the proud horses with their gleaming coats, or admire Wye House, the mansion of the Lloyds. The elegant white wooden building, with its front portico supported by graceful columns, the sweeping drive, the velvety green lawns, the gardens and miles of box hedges, gave Frederick his first glimpse of beauty shaped by man. The windmill with its sweeping sails, and the sloop, the *Sally Lloyd*, breathed an air of freedom into his waking soul.

Frederick's hardships were further softened by his winning two friends. Daniel Lloyd, the youngest son of Colonel Lloyd, singled Frederick out to retrieve his birds when he went shooting. Daniel protected him from the fights of the older boys and brought him cakes from the frequent parties in the great house. Through Daniel's friendship his intelligence was sharpened and some of his slave dialect lost.

Mrs. Lucretia was his other friend. One day when he came howling home after his head had been gashed in a boyish fight, she heard his cries. She invited him into the parlor, an exceptional favor in itself. With her own soft hands she bathed the blood from his head and face and bound his head with a clean cloth dipped in soothing balsam. "Most of all," Frederick recalled, "her kindness was healing to the wounds in my spirit."

Thereafter he took to singing under her window when he was hungry. His usual reward was a piece of bread.

So his own hardships of cold and hunger did not alone account for the intense hatred of slavery that Frederick developed. He could not live long on the Lloyd plantation without becoming sharply aware of what can happen when one man has absolute power over another. Years later he summed up his views, gained from harsh experience:

> The slaveholder, as well as the slave, was the victim of the slave system. Under the whole heavens there could

be no relation more unfavorable to the development of honorable character than that sustained by the slaveholder to the slave.

Shortly after he came to the Lloyd plantation, Frederick had seen his old master brutally repulse the pleas of a cousin from Tuckahoe. The poor girl had hiked twelve miles barefoot and bleeding to beg her master's protection from the drunken overseer, Mr. Plummer. Her neck and shoulders were cut by his whip, her head gashed by a heavy hickory club.

Their old master's answer was Frederick's first lesson in the slaveholder's psychology. "Whatever Plummer did to you, I'm sure you deserved every bit of it. And if you don't get back to Tuckahoe this instant, I'll take the rest of the skin off your back myself."

Frederick soon found that Old Master's cruelty was not confined to words. One morning before dawn, he was awakened in his little closet by the sound of curses, screams, and the sharp cracks of a cowskin whistling through the air. Terrified, he peeped through the spaces between the unplaned boards that separated him from the kitchen. He saw his beautiful Aunt Esther, with her hands tied over her head, seeming to dangle in midair from the rafters. Behind her stood Captain Anthony, flogging her with all his strength.

"Please, I promise! I won't do so no more," Esther cried out. But the captain flogged on for thirty or forty lashes.

At last the kitchen grew quiet except for the sobs of the tortured girl, but Frederick could not sleep. He was to witness —and suffer—other cruelties in his life as a slave, but this first terrible scene remained forever branded upon Frederick's memory. "I never shall forget it whilst I remember any thing. . . . It was the blood-stained gate, the entrance to the hell of slavery, through which I was about to pass."

Once he had walked through that fearful gate, Frederick was exposed to more shocks. The pleasure he had felt at first in the activity and beauty of his new home began to be poisoned. Suppose he was doomed to be a field hand?

He had watched Colonel Lloyd's overseers. First came Mr. Sevier, who never moved but to whip nor spoke but to curse. He died soon after Frederick came to the plantation, and his successor, James Hopkins, didn't last very long. Evidently he was considered too lenient. Most fearsome was Hopkin's successor, the implacable Austin Gore, "who could torture the slightest word or look into impudence," and "had the nerve not only to resent, but to punish promptly and severely."

One day a story circulated through the plantation which froze the blood of every slave for miles around:

Bill Demby was a strong and popular field hand, full of high spirits and a good worker. Somehow he had offended Mr. Gore, who started to flog him. After a few strokes, Bill bolted and dived into the nearby creek where he stood in water up to his neck and refused to come out.

Without moving a muscle, Mr. Gore called him three times to come out. Bill did not move. On the third call Gore raised his rifle, took careful aim, and shot Bill through the head. Bill sank, leaving no trace but a widening pool of blood.

Even Captain Anthony and Colonel Lloyd were shocked by this cold-blooded murder. Colonel Lloyd's face, under his prematurely gray hair, was ruddier than usual as he demanded an explanation of the outrage.

Only Gore remained cool. He explained that Demby had become unmanageable and would have infected the other slaves with his rebellious spirit if he had been allowed to escape whipping. "Law and order" on the plantation would have been at an end. Colonel Lloyd evidently approved this line of reasoning. Gore was not removed from his post; indeed, his reputation for "managing" slaves grew.

As he watched these crimes go unpunished, Frederick was forced to try to make sense of the fact that "God up in the sky" had intended some people to be slaves and some to be masters.

And he must be a slave forever because he was black. He must know no justice but his master's will this side of the grave.

For Frederick, the explanation was not enough even then. His friends and relatives dumbly accepted these bitter facts. He had to ask "Why?"

His doubt was strengthened when his Aunt Jenny ran away with Uncle Noah, one of Captain Anthony's field hands. Old Master was furious and vowed he'd catch them and bring them back. But he never did. The slaves whispered among themselves that the pair had run away to the North to be free.

Apparently, not all black people were slaves any more than the poor whites of Easton and Tuckahoe were slaveholders. Hadn't some of the older slaves told him that they had been "stolen from Africa"?

As he brooded over these things, Frederick began to lose his childish high spirits. The future seemed to darken and close in before his eyes. The songs of the blackbirds mocked him. He would compare with his captivity their freedom to fly where they willed. For what might a plantation slave hope?

3 a mind awakes

A city slave is almost a freeman, compared with a slave on the plantation.

Frederick Douglass

Frederick hurried over the cobblestones of a narrow street along the Baltimore waterfront toward Fell's Point near Gardiner's shipyard. He could still hardly believe the luck that had rescued him from the plantation. He did not understand the economic forces which were pushing the slaveholders of the upper South to hire their slaves to townspeople or sell them south. He only knew that he had been picked from all of Captain Anthony's slave children to come to the marvelous city of Baltimore (then third biggest in the United States) with its teeming streets, closely packed houses, and bustling harbor.

Everything seemed new and strange—his skin scrubbed clean from the grime of the plantation, the new trousers with which Mrs. Lucretia had rewarded him for the first bath he ever took, the dreamlike trip over the waters of Chesapeake Bay, Baltimore harbor with its forest of masts. How could he regret parting from brothers and sisters he had known less than a year? His mother was dead, his grandmother too far away to visit.

Rich, the sailor who led the way, seemed as excited as Frederick about taking him to his new home with Hugh Auld, brother of Mrs. Lucretia's husband, Captain Thomas Auld. As the door opened, Frederick understood why. He saw the face of a white woman beaming at him with such welcome and overflowing kindness as he had never met before.

The lady was Mrs. Hugh Auld, or Mrs. Sophia, his new mistress. Her son, little rosy-cheeked Tommy, danced around him, and Master Hugh gave him a gruff, though not unfriendly, "Hello."

Frederick sidled up to Mrs. Sophia with the fawning smile that he had learned to use to all white ladies, even the friendly Mrs. Lucretia. Mrs. Sophia's warm and open face never changed as he came near. Her eyes drew his despite his effort to keep them downcast.

Mrs. Sophia laid one hand on his shoulder and one on Tommy's, bringing them face to face.

"Tommy," said the new mistress, "here is your Freddy, who'll take care of you. Freddy," she said with another smile, "be kind to little Tommy."

If Mrs. Sophia had asked him to walk barefoot over hot coals, Frederick gladly would have tried it. In fact, his new duties were very easy. Mostly he ran errands for Mrs. Sophia and protected Tommy from rough street boys and runaway carriages and horses.

Public opinion in the city was critical of those who beat or starved their slaves. Across the street from the Aulds were two maltreated slave girls who were a sorry exception to this rule. Frederick, however, slept on a real bed in the kitchen loft, with a straw mattress and blankets. He was well fed and his clothes were clean and well made.

Master Hugh had little time for Frederick. He was too busy "getting on" in the world. As a small shipbuilder in the great port of Baltimore, he worked early and late to build up his business. He left Frederick largely to the care of his wife.

Mrs. Sophia seemed to contradict all Frederick's ideas about how to deal with the white world. She could not seem to get it through her head that curly-haired little Freddy was less than human because his skin was darker than hers and because of certain laws passed by the State of Maryland.

Perhaps it was because she had earned her own living as a weaver and never owned a slave that she had no talent for slaveholding. Perhaps it was because she took her Christianity so seriously.

As she moved about her house, she sang joyous hymns of praise to God. Often, when her husband stayed late at the shipyard and her day's work was done, she would read aloud to Tommy and Frederick from the Bible.

First Frederick was attracted by the stories, then by the book itself. How could those small black lines and circles on the page form themselves into words? Finally, driven by his curiosity and encouraged by Mrs. Sophia's sweetness, he asked her if he could learn to read.

Mrs. Sophia was delighted. Of course her Freddy could learn to read. He was a quick boy with an eager mind. They would start at once on their ABC's.

Frederick proved an apt pupil. The alphabet was completely strange to him, yet he soon learned it well enough to spell out words of three or four letters. His hungry mind, given its first chance to learn, craved knowledge, as his hungry body had craved food back on the plantation.

Mrs. Sophia was very proud of her pupil. She longed to share her success with her husband, but he was so preoccupied. At last one night he came home early, and she told him eagerly of her little school.

Hugh Auld did not return his wife's warm smile. His face grew red and his voice gruffer than usual. In the clearest possible language he forbade his wife to continue in the dangerous course of teaching a slave to read.

"Mrs. Sophia was delighted. Of course her Freddy could learn to read."
(Lithograph, illustrating Douglass's Life and Times, *1892)*

Each word was rapped out like a hammer blow, clamping down the lid on Frederick's newly awakened hopes. "Learning would *spoil* the best nigger in the world. . . . He would at once become unmanageable, and of no value to his master. As to himself, it could do him no good, but a great deal of harm. It would make him discontented and unhappy."

Frederick listened intently to Master Hugh's words—first with surprise, then with a growing gloom, and finally with a sense of discovery. They solved for him the problem that had perplexed him since he had been a boy on the plantation—

> . . . the white man's power to enslave the black man. It was a grand achievement, and I prized it highly. From that moment, I understood the pathway from slavery to freedom.

Maryland was one of the few Southern states where slaves were not forbidden by law to learn to read. Nevertheless, most slaveholders agreed with Hugh Auld that reading was dangerous to slaves. Mrs. Sophia, who began to persuade herself that her husband must be right, would teach Frederick no more.

As Frederick grew older, he divided his time between helping his mistress at home and his master in the shipyard. Master Hugh and Mrs. Sophia could not be always at his heels when he ran errands about the city. So Frederick sought new teachers in the city streets. The poor white boys of the neighborhood were his friends. They all attended the new free school on Bond Street. In exchange for bread from generous Mrs. Sophia's loaf, they were glad to share their newly acquired knowledge.

Perched on a curbstone or a cellar door, the boys would pore over *Webster's Spelling Book* with their young student. Painstakingly Frederick gathered leaves of other books from the "mud and filth of the gutter," and took them home to dry and clean off. Soon he assembled a number of pages of the Bible.

Sometimes Frederick would look at his white friends with

his bright eyes and say, "You will be free as soon as you are twenty-one, *but I am a slave for life!* Have not I as good a right to be free as you have?"

In the natural sympathy of boyhood, they would reply, "Of course you have as good a right to be free as we have. Perhaps you will somehow manage to get free when you are a man."

With the first fifty cents he earned shining shoes in the street, Frederick bought himself a copy of *The Columbian Orator,* a book his friends were using to learn recitations.

He carried it home and hid it in the kitchen loft where he slept. He must keep it from the jealous eyes of Mrs. Sophia, who had grown more suspicious of his reading than her husband. Unaccustomed power over another life had begun to chill her natural warmth.

When Frederick opened *The Columbian Orator* for the first time, he set out on a journey of the spirit from which he never turned aside for the rest of his life. At last he was able to give a name to the doubts and questions that had troubled his mind for so long.

Among his favorite selections was a dialogue between a master and a slave: The slave has run away twice and been each time retaken. When his master accuses him of ingratitude and tells him he has lost the "right of disposing of himself," the slave bravely defends his action:

> I had lost the power, but how the right? I was treacherously kidnapped in my own country, when following an honest occupation. I was put in chains, sold to one of your countrymen, carried by force on board his ship, brought hither, and exposed to sale like a beast in the market, where you bought me. What step in all this progress of violence and injustice can give a *right?*

In *The Columbian Orator,* too, Frederick first read the great speeches of Pitt and Fox, supporting the American colo-

Baltimore in 1830, showing the harbor and waterfront that Douglass knew so well when he worked for Hugh Auld (From an old engraving)

nists during the War for Independence. The heady words concerning liberty and the rights of man were intoxicating to the soul of the young slave.

But knowledge was bitter as well as sweet. Learning at last what freedom meant, Frederick could look clearly at his own degradation. Later Frederick recalled his state of mind in those days:

> In moments of agony, I envied my fellow-slaves for their stupidity. . . . It was this everlasting thinking of my condition that tormented me. . . . The silver trump of freedom had roused my soul to eternal wakefulness. Freedom now appeared, to disappear no more forever.

After all, in Baltimore, there were hints of freedom in the air. As he went back and forth to the shipyard, Frederick met many free blacks who conducted their own businesses, or slaves who hired their own time and were within a breath of freedom. Free Negro sailors visited the busy port, bringing the wind of liberty from the North and the lands beyond the sea.

About this time Frederick began to notice a word recurring in conversations about slavery between Master Hugh and the white workmen in the shipyard. It was a word they would almost spit out—abolitionism. Whenever a slave ran away or stole something from his master or set fire to his house, it was called the "fruit of abolitionism." The Nat Turner rebellion, which occurred in Virginia in 1831, was the most fearful of these "fruits."

In the dictionary Frederick learned only that abolition meant the "act of abolishing." But one day, in the columns of the *Baltimore American*, the mystery was explained. Frederick read that petitions had been presented to Congress asking for abolition of slavery in the District of Columbia and of the slave trade within the United States.

This was precious knowledge indeed. There were groups of people, these abolitionists, who wanted to end forever the cruelties of slavery. More and more Frederick began to feel that he would not always be a slave. Yet he was a *slave for life*. How escape?

White men, Frederick knew from the conversations of his fellow slaves, were not to be trusted, even when they seemed friendly. They had been known to help a slave escape, then capture him and pocket the reward. Soon Frederick would be a man and able to support himself. He must learn to write so he could write his own pass and escape without the help of any white man.

Now for the first time Frederick began to notice the letters the carpenters wrote on the boards they sawed and planed. These marks identified the part of the ship to which each

plank belonged. Frederick soon learned S—starboard (right),
L—larboard (left—now known as "port"), F—forward, and
A—aft. Using a piece of chalk, he traced these four letters on
pavements and fences till he had perfected them. Other letters
he copied from *Webster's Spelling Book*, seeking help from his
white friends.

At night he would sit on his chair in the kitchen loft writing on the spaces between lines in Tommy's old copybooks. The
head of a barrel was his desk.

Sometimes he would hear the sound of a slave coffle,
marching by night to Austin Woldfolk's slave mart on Pratt
Street or to the dock where a ship would bear them far south
to New Orleans or Mobile. The "dead, heavy footsteps" and
"piteous cries of the chained gangs" were infinitely depressing.
They acted as spurs to his ambition.

The Aulds' home was no longer the happy place it had
been when he first came to Baltimore. He had changed and
grown away from them as they had grown cooler toward him.
Mrs. Sophia's anger at his learning was probably aggravated by
the almost sullen thoughtfulness of her once-happy slave boy.
His master, failing in business and drinking heavily, sometimes
threatened to whip him for his dangerous tastes, but never did.
Tommy was becoming the "young Mas'r."

All Frederick's friends now lay beyond the door. Chief
among them was old Uncle Lawson, a free black drayman, who
offered Frederick the consolation of his simple faith in a better
world. At thirteen Frederick was converted and received into
the Methodist church.

Frederick helped Uncle Lawson read his Bible, and
through him met some young men of his race whom he helped
with their letters. Uncle Lawson had boundless confidence in
Frederick. He was convinced his young protégé was destined
to help lift his people from their darkness.

4 **descent into the pit**

So . . . a vast mass of the slaves pass their lives, from the moment they are able to go afield in the picking season till they drop worn out into the grave, in incessant labour, in all sorts of weather, at all seasons of the year . . . .

E. L. Godkin

In the spring of 1833 Frederick Bailey was called back from Baltimore to the Eastern Shore of Maryland, this time to the village of St. Michaels. The call came too soon; he was not yet quite old enough or quite prepared to escape.

Captain Anthony, his old master, had died suddenly several years before, leaving no will. None of his slaves, not even Frederick's devoted grandmother, had been freed. Then, in rapid succession, all Captain Anthony's children died, including kind Mrs. Lucretia, who had inherited Frederick.

By this route, Frederick had passed to the ownership of Mrs. Lucretia's husband, Captain Thomas Auld. Happily for him, Frederick had remained at first in Baltimore. Then Captain Thomas had quarreled with his brother Hugh. In his anger, he had demanded that Hugh return Frederick to him in St. Michaels. Here Captain Thomas kept a store with his second wife, Mrs. Rowena Hamilton, daughter of a local landowner.

Frederick had become a tall, fine-featured lad of sixteen, still slim from his rapid growth. He was put to work in the kitchen with his sister Eliza, his Aunt Priscilla, and his cousin, a poor cripple named Henny.

The fine words of *The Columbian Orator* and the relatively free ways of Baltimore were less than useless to Frederick here. Instead of teaching his friends to read and studying the

great words of the philosophers, he must study the actions and
desires of Captain Thomas and Mrs. Rowena. He must learn
to satisfy those desires.

Captain Auld suffered from all the inconsistencies of a
man who has acquired unexpected wealth and power. His
orders lacked the assurance of a born slaveholder like Colonel
Lloyd. The slaves, especially Frederick, showed their disrespect
by calling him "Captain" still instead of "Master." All the
rages of his coldhearted wife, Mrs. Rowena, failed to enforce
his will. Sometimes he would whip Frederick for his insolence;
next time he would let the same act go unpunished.

Once again Frederick knew hunger. The kitchen staff
must prepare delicious meals for the Aulds while half starving
on cornmeal themselves. Frederick's new powers of reason
came to his rescue. He was justified, he told himself, in stealing
food from his master. He was merely putting one thing—meat
—belonging to his master into something else belonging to
his master—his stomach.

Then, in August 1833, a ray of hope penetrated Frederick's
prison. A religious revival, such as often swept over country
places in those far-off simple days, reached Talbot County.
Tents were pitched in the Bayside. People came from every
town and farm around and from as far away as Baltimore.

Even the slaves were allowed to stand in a narrow space
behind the preacher's pulpit. Frederick suddenly saw Master
Thomas drawn inside the circle. He prayed that his master
might be converted. Master Thomas went down on his knees,
tore his hair, groaned, and shed a tear. All the people said the
captain had "come through."

Not long after, Frederick learned the difference between
the religion of the master and the religion of the slave. A local
white man named Mr. Wilson heard that Frederick could read
and write. He asked Frederick to start a Sabbath school for
slaves.

Frederick was conducting his second meeting when a

mob rushed in upon the class with sticks and stones. It was led by Wright Fairbanks and Garrison West, both religion teachers, and the newly converted Master Thomas. They broke up the school and ordered the teacher and his students never to meet again.

One of the men drew Frederick aside and warned him, "As for you, you're studying to be another Nat Turner. If you don't look out, you'll end up with as many balls in you as he did." (Actually, the leader of the Southampton County, Virginia, rebellion was hanged.)

The Nat Turner rebellion, with its massacre of more than fifty whites, including women and children, had come like a thunderbolt from an angry God upon the people of the South. Nat Turner was said to have been relatively well treated by his master, whose family were the first to be chopped down.

Throughout the South, slaveholders reacted with panic. They passed new laws. It was a crime to teach a slave to read or write. It was made harder, or in some states impossible, to free a slave. It became a crime to publish a newspaper or pamphlet criticizing slavery; criticism might stir up a dreaded insurrection. It was a crime for blacks—slave or free—to meet for any purpose, even religious, without a white man present.

In such an atmosphere, a bright and discontented slave like Frederick Bailey was sure to be eyed more than ever as a troublemaker. One of Frederick's acts of defiance to Master Thomas was his habit of allowing the horse to escape from the barn.

One day, when Frederick came home leading the runaway horse, Master Thomas told him, "I cannot endure your behavior another day. You belong to *me*, and on my farm shall you work. I have determined to put you out to be broken to Mr. Edward Covey. Perhaps there you'll learn what a good day's work is."

For a year Thomas Auld would not have to see this tall,

unmannerly slave whose bold eyes seemed to ask, Why must I be your slave? Am I not as good as you?

Early on the morning of January 1, 1834, Frederick Bailey set out from St. Michaels with his few shreds of Baltimore clothing, now worn thin, tied in a little bundle at the end of a stick. For the first time in his life, real despair began to smother his deep faith that someday he would be free.

That faith had been born long ago when he learned that his forefathers in Africa had been free. It had thrived in the vigorous atmosphere of Baltimore and had even survived his clashes with Master Thomas in St. Michaels. But now he felt himself "but the sport of a power which makes no account either of my welfare or my happiness."

The sight of his new home hardly raised his spirits. It was an unpainted wooden farmhouse which stood near the shore of Chesapeake Bay and had a gloomy pine forest on one side and a sandy waste on the other. A forty-mile-an-hour wind blackened the waves till they were darker than the pines.

More than anything the wind drove him to the door. He had no difficulty in identifying the man who opened the door as Covey himself. Frederick had pictured him clearly from the descriptions of unlucky fellow slaves who had served under him. Covey's venomous gray green eyes, set in a long, wolfish face, darted constantly, suspiciously about as if expecting to see some mischief. His thin, hunched body looked awkward but held the wiry strength of a tightly coiled spring.

Covey lost no time in leading his new hand into the field. For field hand Frederick was to be, now that his master had found him unsuited to work around the house. Frederick, Covey himself, Covey's cousin Bill Hughes, and a hired slave named Bill Smith formed the entire work force to cultivate a farm of three or four hundred acres.

Edward Covey was a poor man who did not intend to stay poor. He understood, as did every poor white man in the South, that land and slaves were the true basis of wealth and

Slaves labor in the cane fields under the eye of an overseer, a fate feared by all slaves of the upper South. (Woodcut by Anderson)

position. Covey rented his farm. In order to attract a steady supply of cheap labor, Covey had built up a great reputation among the landowners of the neighborhood. They knew he could take strongminded, wild young slaves like Frederick Bailey and turn them into hardworking, manageable hands.

Based on his years of experience, Edward Covey had worked out two main ways of controlling the "difficult" slaves who were sent to him to be broken. Frederick was made miserably aware of both of them by the end of the week.

Three days after he came to the farm, Frederick was flogged unmercifully by Covey with hardwood switches. His crime was smashing a gatepost while attempting to drive a yoke of unbroken oxen for the first time.

The weals raised by this whipping were the size of a man's finger. The coarse wool of Frederick's shirt galled the wounds and kept them sore. Before the next week was out, another flogging reopened the scars. During the first six months that he worked in Covey's fields, Frederick was flogged every week with switches or cowskins. His back and limbs continually ached with pain.

Edward Covey's second way of breaking the spirit of his charges was even more effective than his first. During his years as an overseer, he had learned exactly how much work could be done by a man or boy working to the limits of his strength. It was just so much work that he required of every hand who came under his control. He would keep the slaves in constant doubt of his whereabouts and then sneak up behind them with a shout of almost insane glee. So the work went on in his absence as in his presence—dully, mechanically.

Frederick recalled his descent into the pit:

> Mr. Covey succeeded in breaking me. I was broken in body, soul and spirit. My natural elasticity was crushed; my intellect languished; the disposition to read departed; the cheerful spark that lingered about my eye died; the dark night of slavery closed in upon me; and behold a man transformed into a brute!

On Sundays, his only day of rest, he would lie in the shade, his mind blank, a torpor close to coma stealing over his body. At moments an electric spark of hope would race through him, a hard-dying glimmer that restrained him from committing suicide.

A faint whisper seemed to blow back to him from the hundreds of sails winging across Chesapeake Bay. He remembered the pledge he had made to himself from the time he was old enough to understand the meaning of freedom:

> I had as well be killed running as die standing. Only think of it; one hundred miles straight north, and I am free! Try it? Yes! God helping me, I will. It cannot be that I shall live and die a slave.

So Frederick stumbled along till August with his rare flashes of light making the surrounding night seem darker.

Then came one of those hot summer days in Tidewater Maryland when the humidity spreading from the bay seems to press everything to the ground. Frederick was threshing wheat with Bill Hughes, Bill Smith, and another hired slave named Eli. Despite the heat the men worked in a fast rhythm.

Suddenly, about three o'clock, Frederick's head began to turn like the threshing machine. Half blind, Frederick staggered as he gripped a tub full of unthreshed wheat. His head grew heavier till he fell to the ground. With one cog lacking, the winnowing cycle had to stop.

Covey, missing the noise of the flail, ran from the house and found that Frederick had crawled to a corner of the yard to get out of the sun. To Frederick's excuse that he felt sick, Covey answered with a bruising kick in the ribs and a command to get up. Frederick tried to obey, but he blacked out again.

Suddenly a sharp pain pierced the heavy ache of Frederick's head. Covey had struck him with a hickory slat they were using to measure the grain. Blood gushed from the wound, and Covey left, perhaps to get his cowskin.

The sharp sting in his head or the brief rest he had got began to clear Frederick's head. Suddenly he resolved to go to St. Michaels, seek Master Thomas's protection, and beg to be sent to a different master. Before Covey could come back, he limped into the woods.

It was a different Frederick who walked boldly into Covey's yard two days later on Sunday morning, although he had not received any help from Master Thomas. At first his master had seemed deeply moved by the shock of seeing his once-proud slave so battered and bleeding. But prudence, the central core of Master Thomas's character, had soon bottled up this spurt of humanity. Unwilling to lose Frederick's wages for the year, his master had ordered him to return to Covey.

Frederick, however, had not gone back immediately. He

had spent Saturday night with Sandy Jenkins, a shrewd and
warmhearted slave, well known in St. Michaels. Sandy and his
free wife had bravely sheltered Frederick in their cabin and
given him a supper of ashcake. Best of all, Sandy had given
him a magical root. He assured Frederick that no white man
could whip him if he carried this root on his right side.

Frederick was half-ashamed to put any trust in magical
roots. Yet when he surprised Mr. and Mrs. Covey, starting for
church in their Sunday clothes and Sunday smiles, they made
no move to injure him.

As he took his Sunday rest, Frederick felt a new strength
returning to his body. Sandy's kindness and his food—if not
his herbs—along with the unaccustomed two days' vacation,
had left him unusually refreshed. He then and there resolved
that if the root brought no change to the Monday morning,
workaday Covey, he would resist even to the death any further
beating.

Sure enough, on Monday morning Covey's face was as
free of good nature as if he had just breakfasted on bitter alum.
Frederick hurried to the barn and climbed to the loft for the
plow. As he was about to climb down, Covey grasped his legs,
hoping to hobble them with a slipknot.

Frederick leaped before Covey could reach the rope, but
fell heavily to the floor because Covey was still clinging to his
legs. Thinking Frederick stunned, Covey took his time in
retrieving the rope. This was a disastrous mistake. Frederick
looked at the gaunt, bullnecked man with the face of some
predatory bird or animal, who had made his life hell for six
months. A blood madness so great came over him that it blotted
out the whole world of master and slave, black and white.

Frederick dived for Covey's throat and held on until the
blood began to flow under his nails. Now it was Covey's turn
to tremble and cry out in a state of total shock, "Are you going
to resist, you scoundrel?"

"Yes, sir," answered Frederick politely, still keeping him

at arm's length. For two hours Frederick parried Covey's blows, throwing him down on the ground several times. His youth gave him an advantage, but he, too, began at last to tire. Suddenly, Covey dropped Frederick's arms and drew a deep, shuddering breath.

"Now, you scoundrel, go to your work; I would not have whipped you half so hard if you had not resisted."

As he watched the once-dreaded back limping toward the house, a shaken Frederick realized that he had not been whipped at all. A dizzying exaltation came over him. As he wrote in his *Narrative*:

> This battle with Mr. Covey was the turning-point in my career as a slave. . . . I felt as I never felt before. It was a glorious resurrection, from the tomb of slavery, to the heaven of freedom. My long-crushed spirit rose, cowardice departed, bold defiance took its place; and I now resolved that, however long I might remain a slave in form, the day had passed forever when I could be a slave in fact. I did not hesitate to let it be known of me, that the white man who expected to succeed in whipping me, must also succeed in killing me.

In later life Frederick sometimes wondered why Covey never had had him taken to the public whipping post and flogged, as was usually done with recalcitrant slaves. But he suspected that such an action would have spoiled Covey's reputation as a slave breaker. Never again would the local plantation owners have sent him their best young hands to be broken at rock-bottom wages.

Frederick Bailey was never whipped again by Covey, though the baffled slave breaker sometimes growled at him, "I don't want to have to get hold of you again."

To this Frederick's mind answered, No, for you would come off worse in the second fight than you did in the first.

The slave system had no place for a slave who felt this way.

5 a ray of light

The city, with its intelligence and its enterprise, is a dangerous place for the slave.

John S. C. Abbott

Frederick Bailey looked through the narrow, barred window of the jail in Easton, Maryland. By watching the white-jacketed waiters in Sol. Lowe's hotel across the square, he tried to shut out the mocking voices behind him. Frederick's cellmates, John and Henry Harris, sat stoically against the wall.

Those "imps in human shape," the slave traders, swarmed into the cell. They callously felt the strength of each slave's back and arms, poked and punched him to see if he was healthy. All the while they kept up a chorus of taunting questions:

"Ah, boys, we have got you, haven't we? So you were going to escape, were you? Where were you going?"

One asked the young men if they would like him for master. Another said with relish that he'd like to "take the devil out of" Frederick.

Frederick was their special target. More than two years of field work had broadened his back and shoulders, strengthened his arms, and hardened his hands. Though the truth of his fight with Covey was not, of course, known, word had somehow got out that he was "hard to whip." Instead of taming him, his year with the slave breaker had somehow made him seem more defiant, even reckless. This attitude, combined with his ability to read and write, had won the admiration of his fellow slaves.

Frederick and his friends were locked up because, with

Douglass's ancestors had been "stolen from Africa" and brought to America by slave traders like these. (Woodcut by Anderson)

two other hands in a neighboring cell, they had tried to commit the greatest crime in their masters' eyes. They had tried to steal their own bodies—and souls—by escaping. One of their fellow slaves had informed against them. Fortunately, nothing had been definitely proved. They had, by luck and quick thinking, disposed of the passes which Frederick had written to cover their escape. But Frederick's reputation as a troublemaker had led the local slaveholders to believe the worst of him.

It was Easter of 1836. Since January 1835 Frederick had been hired out to William Freeland, a true Southern gentleman, "the best master I ever had until I became my own master." Though hard to please at times, like most slaveholders, Master Freeland was frank and open. He never stooped to deceit.

For the first time since Baltimore Frederick had enough to eat and time to eat it. The slaves worked long and hard at Freeland's, but not before dawn or after dusk. The tools Frederick worked with were the newest and finest available. Best of all he found real friends, almost brothers, in Freeland's slaves, John and Henry Harris. Once again Frederick was able to start a Sunday school, and this one, being kept totally secret, did not suffer the fate of his first.

Why, then, had Frederick often felt discontented? Why did he try to escape? Frederick could explain it very well. When treated like a beast of burden at Covey's, he almost became one. Since Master Freeland treated him as a man, he could think as a man:

> Give [a slave] a bad master and he aspires to a good master; give him a good master, and he wishes to become his own master. Such is human nature.

As they waited for the dreaded footfalls on the steps of Easton jail, footfalls that would mean lifelong separation, Frederick suffered no whisper of reproach from the Harris brothers. They seemed to have no regrets that Frederick had persuaded them of the advantages of freedom with the most eloquent arguments from *The Columbian Orator*.

The dreaded separation came, but not as they had expected. Master Freeland and Master Billy Hamilton, Captain Auld's father-in-law, rode up to Easton right after Easter and had John and Henry Harris and the two hands in the other cell released. They took their slaves home without a single blow or reproach.

Left completely alone, Frederick was forced to look squarely at his probable fate. He was the leader of the escape plot, the truly guilty one. He alone was to suffer the "living death" of the great cotton and sugar plantations or the rice swamps. From that far South, even intelligent and daring slaves could rarely escape.

After Frederick had been in jail a week which seemed a month, Master Thomas appeared one day in his cell.

"You can come home now, Frederick," said Master Thomas. His face was pale and his eyelids heavy as though he hadn't been sleeping well. He seemed really pleased to see Frederick. As they walked out into the bright spring sunshine, which made Frederick's eyes water, Master Thomas continued:

"I haven't known what to do with you, Frederick. The prejudice against you in St. Michaels is very strong, *very strong*. Now a friend of mine is coming from Alabama for a visit. I'm sending you down there with him to work."

After eight years the friend would emancipate him, Master Thomas assured Frederick. The young slave knew of no friends from Alabama. He assumed this was Captain Auld's way of getting rid of him without having to use the despised slave traders.

Several days passed at St. Michaels, and no friend arrived from Alabama. But Master Billy Hamilton rode up to the store one day. In his soft but chilly voice he told Master Thomas to send Frederick away or he personally would shoot the young troublemaker.

Master Thomas well knew that Master Billy was not a man to make idle threats. He decided to send Frederick back to Hugh Auld's in Baltimore, for the brothers had made up their quarrel. There Frederick could learn a trade, and when he was twenty-five, Master Thomas would legally emancipate him! Frederick was jubilant. Baltimore was "the very place of all others, short of a free state, where I most desired to live."

Now that the Auld family had grown cool, Baltimore had new attractions for Frederick. Master Hugh, having failed in his business, had become a foreman in Walter Price's yard. He was able to find Frederick a place as an apprentice caulker at Gardiner's shipyard. On his free Sundays Frederick might mingle with the crowds away from the scrutiny of any master. He would be impossible to distinguish from the free black artisans and workers who were becoming ever more numerous in Baltimore.

The large number of black workers in Baltimore at this time was beginning to disturb white workers. The competition of slaves was driving down wages, as it was in every Southern state. But the white laborers did not think to blame slavery; that would have been "abolitionism." Instead of becoming anti-slavery, the white workers were becoming anti-black.

Just before Frederick went to work in Gardiner's shipyard, it had been the scene of a racist outbreak. Mr. Gardiner had received an order for two men-of-war from the Mexican government. At the height of the rush to complete these vessels by the deadline, the white carpenters had laid down their tools one day. They had refused to go back to work until Mr. Gardiner fired all of his black carpenters.

Because of the racial prejudice, the frantic excitement, and the shortage of carpenters, Frederick found Gardiner's a poor place to learn his trade. Mr. Gardiner ordered Frederick to help any carpenter who needed him. Instead of one boss, he had seventy or eighty. From morning till night he jumped to satisfy their conflicting demands.

As the men grew busier and tempers got short, he would feel the suppressed hatred that had driven the free Negroes from the yard— "Hallo, nigger, come turn this grindstone." "I say, darky, blast your eyes, why don't you heat up some pitch?" Then, three at once. "Come here!—Go there!—Hold on where you are! Damn you, if you move, I'll knock your brains out."

One day, when the hostility of the white workers flared into violence, Frederick had to flee the shipyard to escape being lynched. Master Hugh canceled Frederick's understanding with Gardiner's and took him to Walter Price's yard, where he himself was foreman.

During the year 1837 Frederick worked to learn the caulker's trade. In order to prevent wooden ships from leaking, the caulkers filled the seams between planks with oakum, the hemp from untwisted ropes, or with cotton wicking. Then they sealed the seam with hot pitch to make it water tight. By the end of the year, Frederick had become so skilled with caulking iron and mallet that he was paid the highest wages given to experienced caulkers—$1.50 a day.

At Walter Price's yard free Negroes were still honorably employed. Many of these young men knew reading, writing, and arithmetic. Among them, Frederick could make new friends and could learn as well as teach.

Slaves were generally excluded from the many benevolent societies supported by the free Negroes of Baltimore. But when the free caulkers formed the East Baltimore Mental Improvement Society, they made an exception and asked Frederick to join them in their activities.

At their meetings Frederick took part in his first debates, sharpening his wits and developing his natural eloquence. Among the regular members was a young woman named Anna Murray. Her face was plain and rather stolid, but her appearance was neat and she had about her a sturdy air of independence.

Anna had been born free in Caroline County, Maryland, not far from Talbot County. In her late teens she had come to Baltimore as housekeeper for a rich family. Her quiet confidence was solidly based upon her housekeeping skills and her ability to manage her own affairs.

After so many difficulties and narrow escapes from disaster, Frederick Bailey could stop to count his blessings. He had learned a skilled trade; *that* made him valuable to his master. He had good friends in the shipyard and stimulating company in his free time. He sang in the choir and conducted Sunday school at the Sharp Street Methodist Church. And, most important, he had met a woman more attractive to him than any he had ever known before.

Yet Frederick Bailey's nature would not allow him to be content. "I had grown too big for my chains."

What good did it do Frederick Bailey to earn eight dollars or nine dollars a week? Every cent of it went on Saturday night into the pockets of Hugh Auld. And if Master Hugh gave him nine cents of the nine dollars, he was only admitting that Frederick deserved the whole amount. And of what use to him were the pleasures of his friendships, his religious communion, his learning, if he could be recalled from them at any moment by a whim of his master?

Most important, how could he marry if he could not marry as a man? He could not support his wife. His master might legally break up the marriage whenever he chose.

Anna Murray encouraged Frederick in his desire to escape. She was willing to put her small savings at his command and risk all the dangers and uncertainties of life in the North with a fugitive. And Frederick was more and more willing to throw the dice of chance for freedom again, whatever the cost.

6 new worlds

In leaving you, I took nothing but what belonged to me, and in no way lessened your means for obtaining an honest living. Your faculties remained yours, and mine became useful to their rightful owner. I therefore see no wrong in any part of the transaction.

Frederick Douglass, "Letter to His Old Master"·

Early on the morning of Monday, September 3, 1838, Frederick Bailey drove to the Pratt Street station of the Philadelphia, Wilmington and Baltimore Railroad with Isaac Rolls, a friendly free Negro hackman. Probably only his closest friends would have recognized Frederick that day. Instead of his caulking apron, he was wearing a sailor suit with a red shirt. A tarpaulin hat shaded his face and a black tie was knotted carelessly about his neck. In his pocket he carried a sailor's protection, belonging to a free black seaman named Stanley.

His friend Stanley had lent Frederick his protection at great personal risk, for if caught he was liable to be sold back into slavery. He was but one of a band of heroic and unknown free blacks who thus aided the work of the Underground Railroad. Frederick was to mail back the protection and the clothes upon reaching the free states.

The man described on the protection was about Frederick's height but of much darker complexion. Stanley had warned his friend to avoid buying a ticket in the station where the paper would be closely scrutinized. As the train started to pull out of the station at 6:00 A. M., Frederick jumped aboard. Isaac Rolls flung the bundle to him. It contained his few clothes, his caulking tools, his *Columbian Orator*, his *Webster's Spelling Book*, his hymnbook, and his Bible.

Frederick Bailey settled himself in the car that was reserved for free Negroes. He felt breathless from the events of the past few weeks. He had not planned to escape so soon.

In May Frederick had won from Hugh Auld the right to hire his own time. He was to support himself and buy his own tools, showing himself at Auld's home every Saturday night with three dollars for his master. Living so much as a free man, he began to think as one, too. In early August he had lingered at a camp meeting with some friends outside Baltimore one weekend. He did not present himself to Hugh Auld with his three dollars until Monday night.

Hugh Auld had been convinced that his profitable slave had run away. He grew so angry that he revoked Frederick's right to hire his time. Now that his master was watching his every move so closely and suspiciously, Frederick wondered whether his chance to get free were slipping through his hands forever. He decided to escape at once. Anna had pooled her savings with his and promised to join him as soon as he reached safety in the North.

The train was moving fast for those pioneer days, yet its progress to Frederick seemed agonizingly slow. They were nearing Havre de Grace when the conductor entered the car. The conductor had an abrupt, superior way of speaking; Frederick's heart beat as if a pack of bloodhounds were baying on his trail. Surprisingly, the conductor smiled at Frederick.

"I suppose you have your free papers?"

"No, sir," said Frederick. "I never carry my free papers to sea with me."

"But you have something to show that you are a free man, haven't you?"

"Yes, sir," Frederick replied, "I have a paper with the American eagle on it that will carry me around the world."

A mere glance at the eagle satisfied the conductor. He collected the four dollars fare and continued on his rounds.

Unfortunately the trip involved three changes. At Havre de Grace Frederick joined the other passengers in boarding the ferryboat *Susquehanna,* which crossed the river of that name on the way to Delaware, a slave state.

As Frederick boarded the northbound train, he passed a German blacksmith named Frederick Stein, for whom he had once worked. Frederick whistled a sailor's hornpipe and passed by with head averted. Whether from sympathy or failure to recognize him, Stein never said a word.

Still shaken by his narrow escape, Frederick sat down next to a window. Just opposite him, on the train going south, Frederick saw Captain McGovern, whose revenue cutter he had helped repair a few days before. Fortunately the train pulled out before the captain looked up.

Wilmington was the last stop in slave territory. Here Frederick boarded the steamer *Telegraph* and without a single delay or question found himself sailing across the beautiful Delaware to the "City of Brotherly Love." From Philadelphia he took the train to New York, arriving on September 4.

As a slightly dazed Frederick joined the crowds that, then as now, surged up and down Broadway, a singing exultation lifted his heart. He was free, alone but free. His dearest wish from his earliest childhood was fulfilled. No Old Master, no master of any kind—he was his own master. Frederick wrote Anna that he lived more in one day of freedom than in a whole year of his slave life.

New York was rapidly outstripping all her rivals as the nation's greatest city. Her magnificent natural harbor opened her trade to the fastest ships sailing the Atlantic. The digging of the Erie Canal brought to her docks the rich harvests of Western fields. Irish and German immigrants were beginning to pour through her streets.

But New York was not a safe place for a fugitive. In the carriages that passed Frederick were Southern planters returning from the cool of Northern summers to their plantations. Both business and social relations tied the South to New York, "the northern capital of the Cotton Kingdom."

Fortunately, around noon of that first bright day, Frederick saw a familiar black face. It was "Allender's Jake," who had just escaped from Baltimore.

"Frederick joined the crowds that, then as now, surged up and down Broadway." New York in 1835 (From an old etching and aquatint)

Frederick called him by name. Jake seized his hand, but didn't seem very glad to see him.

"Shhh," he murmured, his finger to his lips. "Call me William Dixon."

Jake set down his whitewash pail and brush. He warned Frederick that New York was almost as much in control of those elegant Southerners driving down Broadway as was Baltimore. He himself had almost been retaken. New York Negroes were not to be trusted. They had been known to betray a fugitive for a few dollars.

Jake warned him especially to stay away from the docks

and the Negro boardinghouses. The human bloodhounds of the slaveholders watched those places closely. He himself could be of no help; he had to go.

Frederick slipped back among the crowds in a more somber mood. The tall brick and stone buildings had impressed him by their grandeur. Now they seemed cold and menacing.

For several days Frederick wandered the streets forlornly, fearing to ask for work or lodging. His little money was soon exhausted. He knew he must find help soon. A friendly black sailor named Stewart, whom he approached, did not seem afraid to be seen talking to the fugitive called Frederick "Johnson." He guided Frederick to the house of David Ruggles, secretary of the New York Vigilance Committee.

The committee was a group of local abolitionists, white and black, who served as the New York station of the Underground Railroad. They helped fugitives escape and protected free Negroes from kidnapping attempts.

Frederick never forgot his debt to Ruggles, that "whole-souled man, fully imbued with a love of his afflicted and hunted people." Ruggles alone aided six hundred runaways over a period of five years. This brave and active man was a writer, printer, journalist, and also the first black bookseller. He founded the first reading room for black people, which was destroyed by fire in 1835.

Ruggles encouraged Frederick to send for Anna. Being free, she came North by train with no difficulty, bringing her small collection of household furnishings. On September 15, 1838, Frederick "Johnson" and Anna Murray were married by the Reverend James W. C. Pennington, who had escaped from slavery in Maryland ten years before.

Since Frederick was an experienced caulker, Ruggles proposed that he and Anna settle in New Bedford, Massachusetts. Many whaling ships were fitted out in that prosperous port. Moreover, it would be safe. Quaker influence had turned New Bedford into an early and active anti-slavery center.

Once in New Bedford, Frederick and Anna were housed and fed by the Nathan Johnsons, freeborn Negroes and Underground conductors. Here they could stay till Frederick found work. Johnson, who was a great reader, suggested to Frederick the name he was to bear ever after. He took pleasure in the idea of naming the tall, noble-looking young man after the hero of Scott's *The Lady of the Lake*, which he had just finished reading. Thus it was that Fred, or Frederick Bailey, Maryland slave, became Frederick Douglass, New Bedford freeman.

The Nathan Johnsons were a revelation to the fugitives. Their home was neater, more attractive, and better run than most slaveholders' houses in Maryland. Nathan Johnson was better educated than the entire population of St. Michaels.

Frederick Douglass was puzzled by prosperous New Bedford. Like most Southerners—white or black—he had been taught as basic truth that all wealth was founded on slavery. Neither the hardworking merchants and sea captains, with their gracious white mansions, nor the industrious workmen, with their snug cottages, fitted this pattern.

Nathan Johnson explained that the exceptionally high level of the black population was due to the schools. In most Northern states Negroes had to support their own schools, although their taxes paid for free white schools they could not attend. In New Bedford white and black children had always attended school peacefully together. Negroes could also vote in Massachusetts as they could in few states outside New England.

Full of hope, Douglass put on laboring clothes five days after his arrival and went down to the docks. Here he helped load a sloop with oil. As he pocketed his first dollar, a solemn feeling of joy welled up in him which no one could understand who had not been "in some sense himself a slave."

Soon after, Rodney French, a rich anti-slavery merchant, offered him a job caulking and coppering a whaling ship. Now he could earn two dollars instead of one dollar a day. As he approached the dry dock where the white caulkers were already at work, the foreman looked up. He seemed surprised and began to whisper with several of the workmen. There was much shaking of heads, and then they all nodded as if a decision had been made. The foreman spoke sharply. "We won't have no darky caulking in this yard." He assured Douglass that if he hammered one iron of oakum into the hull, every white caulker would walk off the job. Deliberately, the foreman turned his back and all his men went back to work as if Douglass were invisible. So there was a line he might not cross even here. He might be a free man, but he was not equal.

These new difficulties did not shake Anna Douglass's rocklike devotion. Despite their reduced prospects for making a living, she settled them comfortably in two neat rooms on Elm Street, overlooking Buzzards Bay. She stood all day at her washboard, taking time off only to collect laundry from New Bedford housewives.

Douglass, though disappointed, was not downcast. A slave was used to hardships. First he took odd jobs, then found steadier work in an oil refinery and a brass foundry.

Even this hot and heavy labor did not discourage Douglass in his quest for knowledge. Four months after he arrived in New Bedford he enrolled in a new school: "Massachusetts Abolition University: Mr. Garrison, president," as he later described it. He subscribed to Garrison's *The Liberator*, the most famous and fiery of all anti-slavery weeklies.

Sometimes Douglass tacked a copy of *The Liberator* to the wall while he worked the bellows which forced air into the furnace. As Douglass explained his state of mind then:

> The paper became my meat and drink. My soul was set all on fire. Its sympathy for my brethren in bonds—its scathing denunciations of slaveholders—its faithful exposures of slavery—its powerful attacks upon the upholders of the institution—sent a thrill of joy through my soul, such as I had never felt before!

Douglass soon had two children to support—Rosetta, born in June 1839, and Lewis, born sixteen months later. Still he remained a laborer, and Anna had to take domestic service when she was able.

Now that Douglass was beginning to live and think as a free man, he found the slights he received because of his color less easy to accept. He left the Methodist church when they served communion to blacks only after the whites had partaken. He joined the Zion Methodist, an Afro-American church, where he became a lay preacher.

He was soon a leader at abolitionist meetings of the articulate blacks of New Bedford. This leadership brought him to the attention of Garrison and resulted in his Nantucket debut.

7 anti-slavery agent

We shall send forth agents to lift up the voice of remonstrance, of warning, of entreaty . . . .

Declaration of Sentiments of the American Anti-Slavery Society

The dancing firelight painted red streaks on the heavy wooden beams of the old farmhouse kitchen. A pretty young girl in a simple gray Quaker gown, poked at the fire, sending a spray of sparks onto the brick hearth. Then she stopped and listened. Outside she heard the crunch of horses' hooves on the frozen ground.

Soon the latch flew up and her cousin Elizabeth Buffum Chace entered. Mrs. Chace was a dignified woman of thirty-five, with her heavy, dark hair pulled severely back, and sad, gentle eyes.

"Our guests are here, Lydia," she said. "We shall need five fresh beds tonight." Then she dropped her voice. An unusual excitement sparkled in her eyes. "I have heard tonight a true miracle—the same fugitive slave that my sister heard on Nantucket. He's here with us now."

Four men and a woman came in with Mrs. Chace's husband, Samuel. The first man, Parker Pillsbury, was a rugged, dark-haired, dark-bearded man, as solid as the New Hampshire granite from which he had sprung. His frequent traveling companion, Stephen S. Foster, was at his side. Though Foster moved awkwardly, his face had a luminous, fanatical beauty.

The woman with them, Abby Kelley, was also dressed in Quaker style. Her sharply chiseled ivory features contrasted with her fire-spitting Irish eyes. Four years later she would marry Foster.

Ignoring the others, the gentle Nathaniel P. Rogers sat down next to the fire and pulled out pencil and paper. He had just been exposed to an exciting phenomenon that was sweeping the anti-slavery societies of Massachusetts. Here is how he described the November 15, 1841, meeting in Providence, Rhode Island, for his Concord, New Hampshire, newspaper:

> . . . fugitive Douglass. . . . This is an extraordinary man. He was cut out for a hero. In a rising for liberty, he would have been a Toussaint or a Hamilton. He had the "heart to conceive, the head to contrive, and the hand to execute." A commanding person—over six feet, we should say, in height, and of most manly proportions. . . . How his owner would cower and shiver to hear him thunder in an anti-slavery hall!

Douglass, who entered last, had been sent into Rhode Island on his most important mission yet. He and his comrades were to denounce a new constitution which would give the vote to all *white* men, but exclude blacks.

Douglass was in company with the toughest—and most extreme—abolitionists in the American society. Even the fugitive slave was a little surprised at some of the language and tactics of Foster and Pillsbury. As ex-ministers they liked to go into churches at sermon time and urge the congregation to "come out" because of the proslavery stand of many church groups and ministers. This technique created a drastic reaction. Usually it was Foster and Pillsbury who "came out"—unwillingly.

"Most all of my time is wasted in getting Stephen out of jail," the slightly more moderate Pillsbury complained of his friend in admiring exasperation.

Pillsbury turned his attention to Douglass. He wanted to hear more of the fugitive's experiences on the Eastern Railroad, of which he had read in *The Liberator*.

Douglass admitted to Pillsbury that the attitude of the

churches was very damaging to abolition and Negro rights. His first run-in with the Eastern Railroad had occurred on September 8 when he and John A. Collins were traveling from Newburyport, Massachusetts, to Portsmouth, New Hampshire.

Four or five brawny trainmen had carried Douglass to the Jim Crow car. As he sat rubbing his bruises, he had been tossed a bone of consolation by the conductor:

"This rule of the directors can't be so bad," he explained soothingly, "for the churches, you know, have their 'Negro pews.' "

"What a commentary on our Christianity!" Collins had concluded his account of the incident for *The Liberator*. Douglass became one of the chief combatants in the paper's running battle with the Eastern Railroad. The degradation of the free Negro of the North grew out of slavery. It must be fought in every form and place where it appeared.

An American railway coach with wood and iron seats like the one from which Douglass was thrown out (From London Illustrated News)

On September 28 Douglass sat with Collins on the wood and iron seats of the "long car" once again, this time on his way from Lynn to a meeting in Newburyport. Opposite sat James N. Buffum, a rich carpenter, very generous to anti-slavery causes.

The train was still in the station when the same "feeble-looking" conductor who had previously ordered Douglass out came slowly down the aisle. The nearer he came to his former opponents the slower he walked. His body trembled visibly and his voice vibrated like a plucked string as he cried, "Out with you, out!" He pointed his shaking finger at Douglass, his eyes all the while on the floor. "You know you belong in the other car."

Douglass answered with great control. "There are but very few in this car. Why, since no one has objected, do you order me out?"

"Let's vote on it," cried one of the spectators.

"Yes, a vote, a vote," echoed others.

"No, no, it's against the rules. Mr. Chase will discharge me. It has nothing to do with votes."

"If you will give me any good reason why I should leave this car, I'll go willingly; but, without such a reason, I do not feel at liberty to leave; though you can do with me as you please, I shall not resist." Douglass had answered in the best tradition of Garrisonian nonviolence.

"You have asked that question before." The conductor was growing peevish.

"I shall continue asking that question over and over again as long as you continue to assault me in this manner." Douglass's voice was a mighty-toned bass against the conductor's thin, fluty tenor.

The conductor studied the toes of his boots; he opened and closed his mouth soundlessly several times. At last he stuttered, "Because you are black." He leaned over and made one futile attempt to pull Douglass out of his seat. Then he rushed for help.

Abby Kelley, later Mrs. Stephen Foster

Soon eight or ten muscular young men surrounded the whole seat in which Douglass and Collins were sitting. They hit Collins on the head when he refused to move. Then they tried to "snake out" Douglass around Collins. But so rooted was Douglass in his place that their straining finally wrenched loose the entire seat.

Disposing of Collins with a kick in the ribs, they carried Douglass and the seat back to the entry. They shoved him to the platform and threw his baggage after him. The kindly Buffum hurried to his side.

Soon Collins, Buffum, and the slightly frayed Douglass were jogging over the rutted country roads to Newburyport in a hired carriage. Within a couple of years, abolitionist pressure on the Eastern Railroad did result in desegregation of its cars.

The next day Mrs. Chace and her husband drove Douglass, Foster, and Miss Kelley to a meeting in Woonsocket Falls.

Here their reception was very different from Providence. White workers had been stirred up at the idea of black men voting in equality with them. A mob of rough men gathered in the back of the hall, well-armed with stones and rotten eggs.

Coarse oaths rebounded through the room as the meeting opened. It was hard to tell what made the mob angrier—the piercing voice of Stephen S. Foster attacking the "Brother-hood of Thieves," as he called the clergy, the idea of a woman speaking in public, or the sight of a Negro sitting on the plat-form. At any rate the mob attacked, scaring away the audience. But the intrepid agents set off calmly for the next town.

Douglass had been an apprentice anti-slavery agent since the end of August. His coolness under such fire as he met at the Woonsocket Falls meeting was one proof that he was no longer a novice.

Douglass's growing mastery of his new profession was shown in another way. His earliest traveling companions, Collins and George Foster and even Garrison himself, used to encourage him by saying, "Just tell your story, Frederick; give them the facts." At first Douglass had been only too grateful to follow their advice.

On November 4, when Douglass had joined Garrison and Wendell Phillips at the Convention of the Old Colony Anti-Slavery Society in Hingham, Massachusetts, he burst forth in a new vein. He attacked the "blood-soaked union," the pledge to return fugitives, according to the best Garrisonian principles. From his own experience he revealed the way in which this pledge discouraged many slaves from trying to escape.

Next he showed how the spirit of slavery had infected the Northern churches. This was a favorite Garrisonian theme, but Douglass gave it a new and graphic meaning.

He described a great religious revival that had occurred not long before in New Bedford. He compared the Kingdom of Heaven to a net that had gathered many souls as if they were fish:

Well, it happened now that some of the fish had
rather black scales; so these were sorted out and packed
by themselves. But among those who experienced religion
at this time was a colored girl; she was baptised in the
same water as the rest, so she thought she might sit at the
Lord's table and partake of the same sacramental elements
with the others. The deacon handed round the cup, and
when he came to the black girl, he could not pass her, for
there was the minister looking right at him, and as he was
a kind of abolitionist, the deacon was rather afraid of giving him offence; so he handed the girl the cup and she
tasted. Now it so happened that next to her sat a young
lady who had been converted at the same time, baptised
in the same water, and put her trust in the same blessed
Savior, yet when the cup, containing the precious blood
which had been shed for all, came to her, she rose in disdain and walked out of the Church. Such was the religion
she had experienced.

Finally Douglass stated for the first time an idea which
was to become central to his fight against slavery and discrimination. It was an idea no other speaker had expressed so clearly:

People in general will say they like colored men as
well as any other, but *in their proper place*. They assign
us that place; they don't let us do it ourselves nor will they
allow us a voice in the decision. They will not allow that
we have a head to think, and a heart to feel and a soul to
aspire. They treat us not as men, but as dogs—they cry
"stu-boy!" and expect us to run to do their bidding. That's
the way we are liked. You degrade us, and then ask why
we are degraded—you shut our mouths and then ask why
we don't speak—you close your colleges and seminaries
against us, and then ask why we don't know more.

For the first time Douglass was beginning to play his own
tune instead of being played upon. Wendell Phillips, that

peerless orator in an age of oratorical giants, noticed it. He whispered to Garrison, "That boy, fresh from slavery, will surpass us all!"

Garrison himself felt it when he rose to say, "Frederick Douglass, though called by slaveholders a *thing*, is, in fact, a miracle! a proof of what a man can do and be in spite of station or condition."

The reporter for the Hingham *Patriot*, who had taken down the speech, conveyed it to his readers. He compared Douglass's ringing defiance and courage to that of the Roman gladiator Spartacus, leader of a slave revolt.

The applause of audiences and the praise of his co-workers increased Douglass's confidence in his latent ability. In January 1842 he was appointed to go before the Constitutional Convention in Rhode Island. The fugitive slave officially protested the use of the restricting word *white* in the new constitution. The word was later struck out.

Douglass hurried from Rhode Island to the annual convention of the Massachusetts Anti-Slavery Society in Boston. Here his fate was to be decided—either he was to become a permanent anti-slavery agent, or he was to return to the obscurity of his life as a New Bedford laborer. John A. Collins's report merely confirmed what everyone already knew, that Douglass was ideally suited to be an agent.

During 1842 Douglass traveled thousands of miles through New England and Upper New York State with his fellow abolitionist agents. He came to know more of the heroic men and women who followed this difficult calling. They had willingly sacrificed comfort, security, worldly position, and the esteem of their neighbors. They had done it because of their belief in the terrible iniquity of slavery. Among Douglass's most frequent traveling companions were the Hutchinsons, Charles Lenox Remond, and the unworldly Unitarian minister, the Reverend Samuel J. May.

Abolitionist meetings were much livelier when Douglass

and his comrades crossed paths with the singing Hutchinsons. The Hutchinsons—Judson, John, and Asa—were part of a musically self-taught family of twelve. Just this year they had persuaded their mother to let their youngest sister, pretty thirteen-year-old Abby, go on tour with them. Often their light, two-horse carriage pulled into a town where Douglass was speaking. Then he could count on an evening of rousing anti-slavery songs sung and composed by the sweet-voiced quartet.

Douglass felt especially close to his new friend, Charles Lenox Remond. A freeborn Negro from Massachusetts, Remond had been the first of his race to travel for the Massachusetts Society. Douglass could learn much from the better-educated Remond, only recently returned from a tour of the British Isles.

Remond was small and dark with thin features. The consciousness that he was the victim of prejudice nagged at him like a persistent ache. Douglass fought "Jim Crow" by direct action. The more sensitive Remond suffered in silent disdain.

In the fall of 1842 the veteran Douglass returned from a tour of Western New York State to Boston. Posters and handbills caught his eye. "Latimer shall go free!" "Agitate! Agitate!" shouted the headlines of *The Liberator*.

Douglass hurried to the dingy room with ink-bespattered windows at 11 Merchants Hall. Here Garrison edited *The Liberator* and wrote his fiery editorials. Douglass looked with awe at the press standing in one corner, the composing stands, and the long editorial and mailing table in the center, piled with unwrapped newspapers. The friendly cat that kept down the mouse population rubbed against his legs.

The grave face of Garrison was alight as he shook Douglass's hand and asked about the success of his tour. But Garrison hardly waited for Douglass's reply. His thoughts were all on the latest sensation—the Latimer case. George Latimer was a fugitive slave, the first ever to be jailed by the state of Massachusetts. Latimer had been seized with no warrant and no evidence but the word of James B. Gray, who claimed to be his owner.

The Garrisonians had requested a trial by jury. They had asked that Latimer be freed on a writ of habeas corpus. Chief Justice Shaw of the state supreme court had denied both motions.

With such encouragement Gray was rushing to reclaim his property. Garrison, meanwhile, was organizing rallies to raise the money to buy Latimer's freedom. Douglass and Remond spoke at a giant meeting at Faneuil Hall, Boston. Then they were sent on to New Bedford and Lynn.

Anna Douglass's usually impassive face lit up when she opened the door to her husband and Remond. Rosetta shouted for joy. Lewis toddled up to him, lisping "Papa." Didn't George Latimer, too, have a wife and child? At Anna's breast nestled the baby, Frederick, Jr., who was but six months old. Suppose Douglass's hiding place were to be found? Suppose Thomas Auld, like James B. Gray, decided to reclaim his lost property?

The cold winds of reality were blowing against Douglass's cozy little home. The walls guarding it, which he had thought secure, were reduced to rubble.

More than any white abolitionist, more even than the freeborn Remond, Douglass understood just what a return to slavery would mean to George Latimer. This feeling burst through every speech Douglass made on behalf of his fellow fugitive.

The marathon meetings in New Bedford and his own nonstop speaking left Douglass with a hoarse throat and a racking cough. He had suffered the first attack of an occupational disease which had finished the careers of a number of abolitionist agents. Douglass fortunately recovered, but for the present he could speak no more.

Nevertheless he accompanied Remond to Lynn. Here he wrote a letter to Garrison describing their successes in New Bedford. The letter concluded:

> I can't write to much advantage, having never had
> a day's schooling in my life, nor have I ever ventured to
> give publicity to any of my scribbling before; nor would I
> now,—but for my peculiar circumstances.

Despite its roughness in composition, the letter caught
something of the power of Douglass's speaking. Garrison
printed it in the November 18 *Liberator*, the first words written
by Douglass ever to appear in print.

By mid-November Gray had agreed to accept four hundred dollars for Latimer, having already spent more than that
in court costs. The agitation produced sixty-five thousand sig-
natures for a petition which the abolitionists sent to the Massachusetts legislature. The result was a new law. State officers
might not be used to catch fugitive slaves, nor state jails used to
hold them.

Latimer joined Douglass on the platform at a great victory meeting in Salem. The light-skinned Latimer could only
murmur an embarrassed thanks. Douglass was the star of the
evening. George Latimer was now free in fact. But it was
Douglass, according to the Salem *Register*, who "was a living,
speaking, *startling* proof of the folly, absurdity and inconsist-
ency (to say nothing worse) of slavery."

8 writing it down

They say the fathers, in 1776, signed the Declaration of Independence with the halter about their necks. You, too, publish your declaration of freedom with danger compassing you around.

Wendell Phillips

In July 1843 two young black men, one small and slim, one tall and broad-shouldered, jolted on the stagecoach into the remote village of Middlebury, Vermont. Charles L. Remond and Frederick Douglass were met by Edward Barber, the only man in town courageous enough to be their host.

As they walked to Mr. Barber's house, they noticed placards on every tree and fence post. Some announced that Frederick Douglass, an escaped convict from the state prison, would address a convention of lunatics, blasphemers, and no-government men who wished to destroy the Constitution. Remond was described in no more flattering terms than his friend.

The students at Middlebury College had been stirred up against the abolitionists by the teachings of their professors. They had mischievously made and posted the signs. In such a cool climate only a few brave souls dared attend their meeting. Nevertheless, Remond and Douglass continued as planned to the next town of Ferrisburg.

Remond and Douglass were the advanced guard of a party of seven agents. They were to organize the One Hundred Conventions in Vermont, Upper New York, and the Midwest during the last six months of 1843.

Upper New York State and Ohio had "received the word" from such men as Theodore D. Weld, Gerrit Smith, and Myron Holley. But these Western abolitionists were mostly practical men, supporting the Liberty party and political action, and working with the Underground Railroad. They had split with Garrison because they disliked his extreme views.

Syracuse was a Liberty party stronghold. On a hot day in late July, Douglass arrived there alone to find that no one would give him a hall. So he spoke in a park where his audience grew from five to five hundred by the end of the day.

The next day Douglass accepted an offer by the Congregational deacons to use their old church building. Whatever their feelings about Garrison and his ideas, the ladies of the local anti-slavery society were quite won over by Douglass. On August 1, they invited him to a fair and supper.

By this time Remond and his old traveling companion, John A. Collins, had joined Douglass in Syracuse. Collins had just returned from abroad where he had been converted to the principles of the French economic philosopher François Fourier. According to his Fourierist principles Collins now believed in the formation of small communities, or "phalanxes," where work and property were shared in common. He spent all his time with his new antiproperty friends.

Douglass was troubled by Collins's indifference to anti-slavery. However, he and Remond were determined to do good work at the fair. These fairs were inspired by the famous Boston Anti-Slavery Bazaar, run each year by the brilliant and beautiful Garrisonian, Mrs. Maria Weston Chapman. They were the great social events of the anti-slavery year.

Douglass and Remond passed among the tables where anti-slavery tracts and wafers (something like Christmas seals) were sold. They admired crocheted pillow covers and doilies and antimacassars and needlepoint samplers on which the ladies sewed all year. Many bore sayings like "God hath made of one blood all nations," and "Men-buyers are exactly on a level with men-stealers."

At the head of the room were tables spread with cold meats and salads, sherbets and cakes, nuts and candies, and tall pitchers of lemonade. As Douglass and Remond were enjoying

Douglass often traveled on a stagecoach like the one shown here.
(Woodcut by Anderson)

the refreshments, the chairman of the evening rose. He announced that Remond would speak on anti-slavery the following afternoon. Shortly after, he announced an antiproperty meeting for the same time and place.

Full of misgivings, Douglass and Remond reached the old church next day. Collins and his friends were already there. When Douglass asked Collins whether they were to hold their anti-slavery meeting that afternoon, Collins quickly showed where he stood.

"I am disappointed in these abolitionists," he said. "They are as bigoted and narrow-minded as other men—for three days they hold a convention opposing chattel slavery, but refuse to devote one day to the abolition of property that enslaves all men."

Collins and his friends shouted that Douglass was "out of order" when he rose to speak. But the audience did not agree. Douglass told them that Mr. Collins had a perfect right to support socialism or any other reform; but, he asked,

> Is it just or honorable to use the cause of anti-property to destroy anti-slavery? If the Board of Managers should sanction such a course, which I do not believe they would, I should feel it my duty to resign my agency in organizing the One Hundred Conventions.

"No, no," shouted the audience as they sprang to their feet, clapping and cheering.

As Douglass left Syracuse he wondered if the board of managers of the society would misunderstand his attack on Collins. Suppose they should take seriously his offer to resign?

Douglass enjoyed a pleasant interlude in the fast-growing town of Rochester, which he had visited the year before. His Quaker hosts, Isaac and Amy Post, added to his warm memories of Rochester.

The booming lake port of Buffalo, his next stop, proved much cooler to his message. In a deserted post office, Douglass worked his familiar magic, building up a large audience from a handful of listeners.

Douglass had been looking forward to this trip to Buffalo. On August 21, 1843, he and Remond watched with interest as the Reverend Amos G. Beman convened the opening session of the National Convention of Colored Men. Douglass was full of anticipation. For two years he had traveled almost exclusively among white men, speaking largely to white audiences, influenced by the white leaders of Garrisonian abolitionism. Remond was his only black friend. Now he found himself among seventy Negroes from a dozen states. Most of them were young; all were among the most articulate and educated of their race. It was like coming home.

Between sessions Douglass sought out the Reverend Henry Highland Garnet, a young man but a year older than himself. Garnet's tall, erect figure, glossy black skin, and strong features proclaimed him the pure-blooded grandson of an African chief.

Garnet had escaped to New York City with his whole

family as a boy of nine. He had attended Charles Andrews's famous school for colored boys. Among his classmates had been actor Ira Aldridge, Professor Charles L. Reason, the Reverend Alexander Crummell of Oxford, and the Reverend Samuel Ringgold Ward.

In 1835 Garnet and Crummell had been accepted as students by Noyes Academy in Canaan, New Hampshire. The citizens of that biblically named town were determined that no black youths should attend school in their midst. They had attached one hundred yoke of oxen to the building, dragged it from its foundations, and burned it. Garnet had finished his education at Oneida Institute for Colored Men and was now a Presbyterian minister in Troy, New York.

Douglass had heard Garnet speak in New Bedford almost three years before. But two years out of Maryland and with the "iron of slavery in my soul," Douglass often felt that his race was doomed to perpetual semiservitude. The sight and sound of Garnet changed all that. It gave Douglass an "exultant feeling" to look upon and listen to this "brilliant contradiction" to all the degrading racist theories that had depressed him.

Douglass was therefore very surprised to see how coolly Remond shook hands with his new acquaintance. Remond took Douglass to meet another young man, whose talents had just been discovered by Garrison.

William Wells Brown was so light of skin that he almost seemed misplaced. Like Douglass he was the son of a slave mother and a white man. Brown's strong resemblance to his master, who was his father, had caused so much comment that he was finally sold. Then he suffered the same kind of cruelties that had embittered Douglass's youth.

In 1834 Brown had escaped into Ohio, where he had become a cook on a lake steamer. He had helped sixty fugitives escape to Canada and picked up an education as he worked. He had just begun to travel for the Western New York Anti-Slavery Society.

The Reverend Mr. Beman's gavel cut short their discussion. He announced that the Reverend Henry Highland Garnet was to give an address. Garnet had named it "Address to the Slaves in the United States."

The "terrible pride" of his chieftain grandfather flashed from Garnet's eyes. Quickly, angrily, he detailed again the kidnapping from Africa, the oppression in America, the destruction of minds as well as bodies:

> To such degradation it is sinful in the extreme for you to make voluntary submission. . . . The diabolical injustice by which your liberties are cloven down, neither God, nor angels, or just men, command you to suffer for a single moment. Therefore it is your solemn and imperative duty to use every means, both moral, intellectual and physical that promise success. . . .

At Garnet's flaming words the audience sat bolt upright to a man. Language like this had not been heard in America since 1829. In that year the mysterious David Walker had published his call for a slave revolt and had been found mysteriously dead soon after.

Douglass was pierced by the excitement in Garnet's voice. He remembered his fight with Covey and his determination to escape. Garnet went on:

> Brethren, arise, arise! Strike for your lives and liberties. Now is the day and the hour. Let every slave throughout the land do this, and the days of slavery are numbered. You can not be more oppressed than you have been—you cannot suffer greater cruelties than you have already. Rather die freemen than live to be slaves. Remember you are four millions.

Clapping, exultant cheers greeted the end of this explosive speech. Douglass, like the rest of the audience, was lifted to his

feet. Then Remond whispered in his ear, "You see, I warned
you Garnet was not to be trusted." This dash of common sense
dampened the fires of Douglass's enthusiasm. He asked to be
recognized by the chair.

With a passion and persuasion equal to Garnet's, Douglass opposed that man's dangerous advice. What good could
come of Garnet's words if they reached the slaves? They might
well inspire to insurrection, and a slave insurrection could only
end in more horrors visited upon the slaves.

Douglass proposed a resolution, seconded by Remond
and Brown, that Garnet's speech be rejected on the grounds
that it was warlike and encouraged to insurrection. So powerful
had been Garnet's appeal that the resolution was only carried
by one vote.

Nevertheless, Douglass received many congratulations on
his masterly speech. His great influence among his people dated
from that moment. He was refreshed and encouraged when he
rejoined his white friends in Ohio.

Fall was coming as they crossed into Indiana. The cool
nights matched their increasingly chilly receptions. Many Indiana farmers were Southern by birth and hated abolitionists.
Douglass and his white companion, William A. White, were
heckled and pelted with eggs at their first meeting in Richmond.

In Oakland on September 8 Douglass was greeted by
coldness and distrust from a more distant source. Mrs. Chapman, who was on the board of managers of the Massachusetts
Anti-Slavery Society, wrote a letter scolding him for insubor-
dination to his superiors in his criticism of John A. Collins in
Syracuse.

The patronizing tone of Mrs. Chapman's letter was deeply
insulting to Douglass's growing independence of mind. The
intellectual and aristocratic Mrs. Chapman was one of those
white abolitionists who wished to do all the thinking for her
Negro colleagues.

Remembering his debt to Garrison and Phillips, Douglass answered her as politely as he could:

> I do not think you would have felt yourself called upon, did you know me as many others do, to have said anything to me, of the Board, entitling them to my gratitude and respect. I trust I have, as far as one can have, a just sense of their claims to my gratitude and respect.

Douglass may have felt better when he discovered that his new friend Garnet had also been hit by one of Mrs. Chapman's shafts. Garnet had answered that since he had escaped from slavery, "It . . . astonished me to think that you should desire to sink me again to the condition of a *slave*, by forcing me to think just as you do."

Soon Douglass was facing more immediate hardships. On September 15 he and White reached Pendleton, Indiana, in a drizzle. When they inquired for the house of Dr. Russell, their host, they were greeted by surly, laconic answers. They were followed part way to his house by scowling horsemen, who had been clattering back and forth along the muddy street. Unfriendly eyes peered through the half-closed curtains of the frame houses.

Dr. Russell explained that sympathy for slavery was strong in Pendleton. He had been unable to find them a hall.

The next morning Douglass and White helped Russell and his handful of abolitionists erect a wooden platform in a nearby forest. The sun was shining, but the mood of the crowd was doubtful.

Mixed with the curious and interested spectators were the unshaven men in buckskins who had eyed them so belligerently the afternoon before. There seemed to be dozens of them.

White had no sooner stood up to open the meeting than one of the biggest and meanest members of the mob threatened him with a pistol. The bully announced that no one was

going to speak that day except him. His minions began to howl and shriek behind him. Some started tossing eggs and brickbats.

Then Douglass stood up. The sight of him was the last straw to the mob. They stormed the platform and began to strike at it with clubs and axes. Their ringing blows splintered the wood. Sticks and stones rained on the abolitionists. Seeing the odds so heavy against them, Douglass was about to beat a wise retreat with Dr. Russell and his wife.

Then a cry went up, "We got him!" and he thought he saw White felled by a heavy stone. Forgetting his nonresistance principles, Douglass seized a club dropped by one of the bullies. He dashed into the hottest, noisiest part of the fray. At least ten men rushed him, tearing the club from his hands. They began to pound at him with their clubs, shouting, "Kill him! Kill the nigger!"

A blow struck Douglass's hand with such impact that the bone snapped. A dagger of pain shot through his arm, wiping out his consciousness. He fell to the ground. Fortunately, White had not been knocked out, though he had lost several teeth. He rushed back to wrest the club from a tall brute who was preparing to give Douglass the death blow.

As suddenly as they had come, the whole band remounted their horses and rode away like a rising gale. Most of the spectators had been frightened away. But a kind Quaker farmer, Neal Hardy, took the unconscious Douglass home to his wife. Mrs. Hardy bound Douglass's hand, but since it was never properly set, it never regained its old dexterity.

The stunned, crippled Douglass and the somewhat battered White showed the resilience of true abolitionists. They spoke the next day in the next town.

"At least ten men rushed him, tearing the club from his hands."
(Lithograph, illustrating Douglass's Life and Times, *1892)*

By November Douglass had rejoined Remond and Sidney Gay, another white agent, in the friendlier precincts of Ohio. They made the trip over the Alleghenies into Pennsylvania on horseback. Wherever they went, people "wanted to hear Douglass," as his companions reported to the newspaper. Remond, morose at times, was beginning to resent his friend's popularity.

Soon Douglass's growing powers of expression began to create a more serious problem than Remond's jealousy. Perhaps Collins had been right to warn him to "keep a little of the plantation speech."

In 1844 Douglass toured triumphantly all over New England and the main cities of the East. As he left the platform, he was likely to hear some hardheaded Yankee exclaim, "He's never been a slave, I'll warrant you." Soon *The Liberator* was receiving letters that raised the same doubt.

Douglass knew that such reports, if they continued, could destroy his effectiveness as the voice of his brothers in bondage. But his mind was taken up with family affairs toward the end of 1844.

He was moving his family into a new house that he had built himself. It was in Lynn, Massachusetts, not far from the street where the singing Hutchinsons' brother Jesse kept a store. Lynn was a hotbed of abolitionists at the time, and closer to Boston than New Bedford.

Shortly after they moved into the house, Anna gave birth to her fourth child, Charles Remond. As a gift to his wife, Douglass announced that he intended to spend the winter at home. Rosetta, Lewis, Frederick, and baby Charles could romp with their father each night.

Douglass had decided that the only way to remove the doubts of his admirers about his origins was the simple but dangerous way of telling the whole truth. He, a self-taught slave, must write a true biography of his whole life up to his discovery at Nantucket.

Wendell Phillips, aged 30

Writing proved the hardest work Douglass had attempted since he had struggled over Tommy Auld's copy books back in Baltimore. But soon the memories came almost too fast and sharp; they flowed from his pen with surprising ease.

Douglass did not base his *Narrative* only on his own harrowing experiences. He wished to draw up a searing indictment of all slavery. So he showed how common were cruel floggings, the impunity with which a slave could be murdered, the poor food, skimpy clothes, and crowded, dirty quarters of the slaves.

One day in April 1845 Douglass took the train from Lynn to Boston. No one any longer questioned his right to ride first class. He walked down Essex Street to a plain, narrow, three-story brick house. He was shown up to a second-floor library, decorated only with books.

A handsome man in his thirties paced before a cheerful fire. His reddish blond hair was starting to recede from his fine, high forehead, giving him a thoughtful air.

"Sit down, dear friend," he said, pointing to a comfortable chair near the hearth. "I am 'all ears' to hear your story and yet I am afraid to know the truth. I have always advised you to keep these dangerous facts as secret as possible."

It was to the most literate of the abolitionists, Harvard-educated Wendell Phillips, that Douglass had chosen to read his *Narrative* for the first time. Phillips had endeared himself to Douglass not only for his learning, but also for his courage and his kindliness.

Douglass also admired Phillips because he was one of those rare men who lived completely the principles he preached. If Douglass were forced to ride in a "Jim Crow" car, Phillips would insist on riding with him. If Douglass had to spend the night on a steamer deck with the cattle and sheep, Phillips would wrap himself in his elegant greatcoat and sleep at his side.

For several hours thereafter, nothing was heard in the study but the snap and hiss of the burning logs and the deep, rolling music of Douglass's voice. When he finished there was utter silence. Even the fire had sunk to a burning log, and a spring damp crept from the corners of the room. Outside, dusk had begun to fall.

"Burn it; you must burn it at once," said Phillips suddenly to Douglass. "It is not safe, and you are not safe. To think that in Massachusetts, an honest man may not tell his name." Phillips's voice conveyed the same urgency that so transfixed his listeners when he spoke in Faneuil Hall.

Douglass then assured Phillips he was determined to publish his story; otherwise his usefulness as an anti-slavery lecturer was at an end.

"I see you have made up your mind," said Phillips. "Well, perhaps after all, we can protect you here in Massachusetts, where a few brave men place the law of God above the laws of men."

Phillips then suggested that, partly for his safety, partly

for the good of the cause, Douglass cross the Atlantic to Great Britain. The warm friends of abolition there had met Remond, but never had they beheld a fugitive slave in the flesh.

In May 1845, Phillips proposed a resolution at a meeting of the New England Anti-Slavery Society. It welcomed to the ranks "the new anti-slavery lecturer, author of the *Narrative of the Life of Frederick Douglass, an American Slave.*" Barely published, the book was already selling like hotcakes. Letters poured in telling how the book filled anti-slavery workers with new understanding and enthusiasm. The New York *Tribune* called it an excellent proof of the "powers of the black race."

Amid all this acclaim, it was well for Frederick Douglass that his ticket was bought and his sailing date set for August 16. Wendell Phillips had written English friends how much they would enjoy meeting the "most remarkable and by far the ablest colored man we have ever had here." The profit from the *Narrative* and the care of the good ladies of the Boston and Lynn anti-slavery societies would safeguard Anna and the children.

Already in far-off Maryland Thomas Auld had begun to hear rumors of the location of his "runaway chattel," Frederick Bailey. His most troublesome piece of property had resurrected to haunt him again.

9 adventures abroad

Liberty in Hyde Park is better than democracy in a slave prison—monarchical freedom is better than republican slavery—things are better than names. I prefer the substance to the shadow.

Frederick Douglass

The promenade deck of the steamer *Cambria* pitched and rolled in the heavy swells that can agitate the North Atlantic even in summer. Gentlemen and a few ladies strolled back and forth in the shadow of the great steadying sail. They stopped at times to exchange polite questions about the weather and the state of their health. Suddenly, health and weather were forgotten.

There were murmurs—some of interest and some of shock. Up through the door that led to the crowded steerage of the boat came a party of six that riveted all eyes. There was a pretty young girl not more than sixteen. The young girl strongly resembled three of the young men, who had flowing locks almost as long as hers, and loose, poetic white collars. There was a bluff, hearty, middle-aged man. The last to emerge was a black man, tall and commanding.

The four young Hutchinsons had recovered from the seasickness of the first few days aboard and had gone to the steerage to bring their friends, James Buffum and Frederick Douglass, up on the promenade deck. Buffum had tried to get cabin passage for Douglass, but in vain. The Cunard Line feared to lose the trade of Americans if they did not bow to the American prejudice against color.

Several American ladies turned their parasols to shield their eyes from this outrageous sight. But most of the people looked up with interest at this promise of amusement.

Soon little knots of people were discussing slavery and abolition all over the boat. The *Narrative*, which the Hutchinsons were peddling on the upper deck, was enjoying a brisk sale.

Bluff Captain Judkins was very interested in Douglass's story. He was glad Queen Victoria had abolished slavery from British possessions—it was a great sin, though he admitted to having once owned slaves. When a number of passengers asked to hear Douglass, the captain called a meeting for the Wednesday evening before they docked in Liverpool.

Some of the passengers had already drunk a good deal of champagne in celebration of landing. Just then a bell summoned them to a meeting on the saloon deck. They found Douglass standing in front of the mainmast.

A rumble of anger arose from the group that was most flushed with wine. Why had they been called from their revels to hear a black man speak? The noise grew so loud that the Hutchinsons broke into one of their most soothing and popular songs:

> Behold the day of promise comes,
>   Full of inspiration,
> The blessed day by prophets sung
>   For the healing of the nation!
> Old midnight errors flee away
>   And soon will all be gone,
> And the heavenly angels seem to say
>   The good time's coming on.

For a moment, the plaintive sweetness of their air, "like the angel of old, closed the lion's mouth." In this temporary lull Douglass tried to begin his speech. He requested the "kind passengers of the *Cambria*" to consider the sad plight of three millions of his brothers in bondage. Immediately, a stiff-jawed Connecticut clockmaker named Hazzard shouted, "It's a lie!"

Douglass, unruffled, spoke steadily on. He told his audience that the slaves were denied the blessing of learning to read the Bible. Hazzard again snapped out, "It's a lie."

"You see, honored ladies and gentlemen," said Douglass, "Mr. Hazzard has good reason for his puzzling conduct. In America the colored man is treated as a thing—without the rights of a man."

"Stop him! Stop him! He's insulting his country!" Several of the younger men closed around Douglass, shaking their fists under his nose.

"Throw him overboard! Throw him overboard!"

"I wish I had him in Savannah! I'd use him up!"

The captain strode up. "Gentlemen! Gentlemen! Have the courtesy to allow Mr. Douglass to continue. I try to make all my passengers happy, and there are many who wish to hear him speak. Those who do not can easily go to another part of the deck. Pray proceed, sir," he said, turning to Douglass.

The rumble of discontent died down while the captain spoke, but resumed with greater fury as soon as Douglass opened his mouth.

"Stop that speech! Throw the captain overboard, too!" one man shouted unwisely.

The captain's bóiling point had been reached. "Send the bos'un for the irons and seize that man!" The irons were actually brought, and the sight of them had a sudden sobering effect upon the mob. But Douglass, realizing he could not speak that day, had quietly, sadly returned to steerage. He wondered if, after all, his reception in England would be so different from that in America.

By September 1 Douglass and Buffum had parted from the Hutchinsons and crossed the Irish Sea to Dublin, where they were welcomed by the local anti-slavery agent, Richard D. Webb. Douglass need not have worried about his reception in the British Isles. He was fortunate enough to be arriving in the afterglow of the romantic period. Not many years before, men like Lord Byron had gone out to fight all over the world for the rights of man. Reform was in the air.

In 1833, after a long fight, slavery had been abolished in the British colonies. Six years later the British and Foreign Anti-Slavery Society had been formed to combat slavery and the slave trade all over the world. Universal suffrage, universal peace, temperance, the rights of workingmen—all were being preached with enthusiasm.

Ireland was standing on the brink of her worst potato famine, the one that was to drive millions of her citizens to America. But the misery he beheld in no way dampened the warm hospitality Douglass received.

At first Douglass entered churches or hotels or hailed cabs a little gingerly. But the cabbies stopped gladly at his bidding. No one prevented him from entering any building. No one scowled when he shared a theater seat or church pew. No one moved away if Douglass sat down next to him in a restaurant or railway coach.

Douglass wrote a letter to *The Liberator* summing up his stay in Ireland. Never once since landing had he heard the mocking refrain that dogged his footsteps in every public place in America, *"We don't allow 'niggers' in here."* Only American tourists had looked disapprovingly upon his visit to the palace of the Marquis of Westminster the day after he landed in Liverpool. This prejudice "sticks to them wherever they go," he noticed. "They find it almost as hard to get rid of as their own skins."

Douglass, breathing a more liberal air, learning every minute, began to be attracted to some of the universal reforms that other Garrisonians had long supported. One of the first to attract him was the temperance crusade. Douglass still remembered how Master Thomas, Master Billy, and the other slaveholders had encouraged their slaves to get drunk at Christmas. It was another means of degrading the slaves by depriving them of their manhood.

Daniel O'Connell, "The Liberator," in his prime

As he walked through the streets of Dublin, beggars swarmed around him. When, his heart pierced by their rags and dirt and degradation, he gave them a few coppers, they would not leave him alone. Wherever he went, they swarmed about him, shaking stumps of arms and legs, staring from blind eyes, holding up miserable infants too weak to cry. Not since he left Lloyd's plantation had he seen such bleak hovels as those of the Irish poor. Men, women, and children lay down together in the same confusion as in Lloyd's "long quarter."

Everywhere about the poor, more piercing than the stink of decay, dirt, and human and animal waste, was the smell of liquor. Douglass was unversed in the economics that would have explained the plight of the poor Irish laborers, driven from their farms by the harshest tenant system in Europe. To him it seemed that liquor was the cause, not the consolation, for their poverty.

Happily he joined in Father Matthews's crusade to sign up the poor to the "cold-water pledge." With his help one thousand signed it in one night.

Then, one day after he had been in Ireland for several weeks, even the ragged throngs limping over the cobblestones began to dance. "There goes Dan! There goes Dan!" cried a group of street urchins, their rasping little voices softened by an immense devotion. A few minutes later Douglass beheld for the first time Daniel O'Connell, the "Liberator." O'Connell had fought long and hard for Catholic emancipation and equally hard, though in vain, for the repeal of the union between England and Ireland.

A great meeting was announced for Conciliation Hall on September 29, 1845. O'Connell was to speak in favor of repeal. Douglass and Buffum were among the seven thousand who crammed the great hall. Though they were far back, the thunder and sweetness of the grand old man's voice reached them perfectly. Douglass was completely captivated by the great-souled leader. He was a friend to all the oppressed, including the slave. O'Connell finished speaking and took his seat. There was a tempest of applause, followed by a reverent hush.

Now that their hero had finished, some of the audience tiptoed from the hall. Hoping to get a closer look at the great man, Douglass and Buffum walked down the aisle to find vacated seats closer to the platform. Many eyes followed the striking figure of the Negro orator.

Taking advantage of this interest, James Buffum tapped John O'Connell, the "Liberator's" son, on the sleeve. O'Connell introduced Douglass, who was immediately asked to go to the stage.

Regent Street, London, in 1842, looking toward the Duke of York's Column (From T. S. Boys, Views of London)

Daniel O'Connell stood up to grasp Douglass's hand with a fervor age had not destroyed. O'Connell then led off with a denunciation of slavery that would have sounded quite at home in Faneuil Hall. He would, he said, "never purchase the freedom of Ireland with the price of slaves." To the sound of cheers he introduced the "black O'Connell of America."

Douglass was speaking for the first time to a large audience abroad. They had come not to hear slavery denounced but to listen to one of the most magical orators golden-tongued Ireland had ever produced. Yet Douglass created a great wave of enthusiasm for his own words and cause.

By the time Douglass crossed to England and Scotland in the winter of 1846, his fame was already going before him. His old enemies, the *Cambria* mob, had unintentionally helped spread his name over the British Isles. On landing they had unwisely attacked him in the newspapers. Immediately the newspapers had sprung to the defense of the fugitive slave. They had expressed shock both at the segregation practices of the Cunard Line and at the cowardice of the mob that had tried to stop Douglass from speaking.

Douglass was to spend nearly two years in Great Britain. During that time he was to grow from the best-known black abolitionist in America into a worldwide symbol of the potential of his people. He did much to keep anti-slavery sentiment aboil in England. He also grew in mind, in spirit, in effectiveness of speech, and in external polish of manner. His hunger for education led him to visit every historic and cultural monument in Britain.

In England he was invited to sit in the privileged Speaker's Gallery of Parliament. In America, he pointed out in one of his letters home, if he had tried to take a seat in the public gallery in Congress

> the ardent defenders of democratic liberty would at once put me in prison, on suspicion of having been "created contrary to the Declaration of American Independence." On failing to provide a negative, I should be sold into slavery, to pay my jail fees.

In England Douglass was greeted by lord mayors and ministers and members of Parliament like Lord Brougham, Robert Peel, and the great reformers John Bright and Richard Cobden. In America many mayors refused even to allow him to speak in their towns.

In England Douglass was entertained at the homes and dined at the tables of the "best people." John Bright invited him to meet his sisters. William and Mary Howitt, editors and writers, had him as house guest for a number of days. He made friends among the educated people active in good causes, like

Henry, Anna, and Ellen Richardson and Julia and Eliza Griffiths. In America even his abolitionist friends sometimes hesitated to walk with him on the street for fear of being mobbed.

In May 1846 Douglass came down to London from Scotland. The breathless schedule he faced was typical of his British tour and his widening reform interests. He spoke on suc-
cessive days to an anti-slavery meeting, a peace meeting, a
"complete sufferage" meeting, and a temperance meeting. The
high point was his speech at a huge public meeting called in
his honor at Finsbury Chapel.

For three hours the crowd hung on his words. Sometimes
they were hushed by his spell. Sometimes they grew stormy
with applause. Douglass answered the question about his tour
that had been raised by many American newspapers unfriendly
to abolition. Why had he come to Britain to attack American
slavery? His answer was that slavery was "the common enemy
of mankind." Moreover, it was an evil so poisonous that it had
sapped the moral strength of Americans to rid themselves of
it. "It requires the humanity of Christianity, the morality of
the world to remove it," he said.

At the end of his speech the enthusiasm was so great that
George Thompson, the British abolitionist, quickly raised
$450. He offered it to Douglass for the purpose of bringing
over Anna and the children and settling permanently in Britain. The offer was very tempting. Life in Britain was so pleasant. But Douglass felt that duty required him to return home.

Douglass was very lonely that summer of 1846. Buffum
and the Hutchinsons sailed home. He missed Anna and the
children more and more. Wandering the narrow back streets
of London Douglass saw a violin in the window of a second-
hand shop. He bought it, took it to his hotel room, and taught
himself to play it.

Then William Lloyd Garrison arrived and had need of
his protégé. With Garrison and the single-minded eccentric
Henry C. Wright at his side, Douglass was drawn into more

meetings and more reformers' battles than ever. Garrison was hailed everywhere by British admirers.

Douglass's most memorable day with Garrison, however, was a quiet one. Joined by George Thompson, they visited Thomas Clarkson, the grand old man of the British Abolition Movement. Once Clarkson had traveled the length of the coasts of Britain, Africa, and the West Indies. He had recorded the horrors he saw in his great work on the African slave trade.

Though eighty-six years of age and very feeble, Clarkson greeted them fervently. He clasped Douglass's hand and spoke to him in a voice trembling with emotion.

"God bless you, Frederick Douglass! I have given sixty years of my life to the emancipation of your people, and if I had sixty more they should all be given to the same cause."

Seeing his great weakness, the three younger men soon bade him farewell. But Douglass carried away the stirring memory of this meeting of two centuries of dedication to abolition. Within a month Clarkson was dead.

Garrison left England in early November. Douglass, Thompson, and Webb led the cheering on the dock. As Douglass watched the sails slip over the horizon, he felt a wave of still greater homesickness. He had hoped and planned to go home with Garrison. But Garrison insisted he was doing the cause too much good to leave. He should stay six months longer. Besides, there was great danger now if he returned.

The revelation of his true identity had indeed reached the ears of Master Hugh and Master Thomas. They were furious to learn that their former chattel was going about the North denouncing them for their meanness and cruelty. Thomas Auld had transferred the ownership of "Frederick Bailey, or Douglass" to his poorer brother Hugh. And Hugh had instituted proceedings to reclaim his lost property.

Douglass was troubled by another problem during his months abroad. It was the friction growing out of the patronizing air assumed toward him by some white abolitionists. He did not mind Garrison's own attitude. As the leader, Garrison assumed command with all of his followers, whatever their color. However, Douglass was growing less patient with the attitudes of some other Garrisonians.

Mrs. Chapman was once again the immediate cause of his irritation. She wrote Richard D. Webb, the Irish agent, to watch Buffum and Douglass to be sure they were not "bought up" by the London abolitionists unfriendly to Garrison. She was not as worried about Buffum, who was rich, as she was about Douglass, who was poor. Webb tactlessly showed the letter to Douglass.

Douglass wrote her, politely but firmly expressing disappointment at her lack of confidence:

> Of one thing, I am certain, and that is I never gave you any just cause to distrust me, and if I am watched over for evil rather than good by my professed friends, I can say with propriety, save me from my friends, and I will take care of my enemies.

Later in the letter he assured Mrs. Chapman that the incident would not disturb their friendship. Yet, even four years later, Douglass wrote Webb that her suspicions had preyed on his mind.

The misunderstandings with Mrs. Chapman were the underground bubblings of a volcano that was one day to erupt. Douglass's more immediate problem was solved in a most gratifying way. The Richardsons raised seven hundred dollars among his many English friends to buy his freedom from Hugh Auld.

In December 1846 his friends placed in his hands the precious paper, in which Hugh Auld, in consideration of the seven hundred dollars, declared that:

> FREDERICK BAILEY, otherwise called DOUGLASS, being of the age of twenty-eight years, or thereabouts, and able

Mrs. Maria Weston Chapman

to work and gain a sufficient livelihood and maintenance
. . . I do declare to be henceforth free, manumitted, and
discharged from all manner of servitude to me, my execu-
tors, and administrators forever.

Douglass was doubly pleased by this great gift because
he would never have asked anyone to pay a penny to the "man-
stealer" who had owned him. Every danger which had over-
shadowed the prospect of seeing Anna and the children blew
away like smoke.

Then new clouds blew over, much to his surprise. Garrison himself had gladly contributed his "mite" to help free his friend from danger. However, many abolitionists were shocked by the transaction. For several months the columns of *The Liberator* buzzed like a wasps' nest in which anti- instead of proslavery workers did the stinging. It was wrong to trade in human flesh, they insisted, even to save a man from danger of death. From the high-minded Garrisonian view, the people who decried the purchase may have had logic on their side.

Douglass, however, was a practical man and was beginning to chafe more and more at the Garrisonian straitjacket. He preferred to look at slavery in human, rather than philosophic, terms. To him the purchase was "ransom paid to a pirate."

Duty called him to go home, he announced at a great testimonial dinner given at London Tavern by his friends. In his farewell speech, he explained why he had rejected the peaceful haven of life in England:

> I prefer living a life of activity in the service of my brethren. I choose rather to go home; to return to America. I glory in the conflict that I may hereafter exult in the victory. I know that victory is certain.

As the distinguished audience rose to its feet cheering, Douglass could measure the degree of his success in England. New dreams and projects were forming in his mind: $2,100 was being raised in testimonial funds to enable him to start an anti-slavery project of his own choosing.

Douglass understood the difficulties he faced. Once again he would have to relearn all the degrading rules of segregation in the country he was too proud to desert. Before he set foot on American soil, he had already bumped against them. The Cunard agent in Liverpool refused him passage on the *Cambria* unless he agreed to take all his meals alone.

In parting Douglass sent off an indignant letter, describing his treatment by the steamship company. The *Times* printed it on April 7. It set off such a hue and cry among British papers that Mr. Cunard had to answer it. In his reply he promised that never again would his ships discriminate against passengers because of color.

As Douglass sailed home in his enforced solitude, he at least enjoyed the rest he needed. He could look forward to a busy life. He would press the attack against slavery ever harder because, as he was to explain in a speech on his return:

> The conscience of the American public needs this irritation. *And I would blister it all over, from center to circumference,* until it gives signs of a purer and better life than it is now manifesting to the world.

To fight the great evil more effectively, Douglass hoped to bring up a new weapon. The money his English friends were raising would help him, the unschooled ex-slave, to start his own newspaper. He would work to make it a model of what a black man could accomplish. He could hardly wait to tell Anna of his new plans.

10 **editor at work**

. . . the man who has suffered the wrong *is the man to* demand
redress— *. . . the man* STRUCK *is the man to* CRY OUT—*and
. . . he who has* endured the cruel pangs of Slavery *is the man to
advocate Liberty.*

Frederick Douglass, *The North Star,* December 3, 1847

The applause that greeted his return from England was still
ringing in Frederick Douglass's ears. His health had been
toasted, in nonalcoholic punch, by half the anti-slavery societies in the East. His great success abroad had brought him
greater fame at home.

Though pleased, Douglass was thinking more of his new
project than of the fact that his name alone could now fill a
hall. He had just come to the anti-slavery office in Boston to
outline his plans for Garrison and Phillips.

"My dear Douglass, I am horrified," declared the elegant Beacon Street voice of Wendell Phillips. "Why, this
paper will utterly ruin you in three years! Your family will be
reduced to beggary!"

Garrison launched his attack by asking why another abolitionist newspaper was needed. "Are not *The Liberator* and
Anti-Slavery Standard enough?"

"But," Douglass put in mildly, "these papers are not
written and edited by colored men. Think what a stunning
answer to the slaveholders and their Northern apologists—to
have a well-edited, well-written, attractively printed newspaper,
put out by a Negro."

"There may be some merit in what you say," remarked
Garrison, hardly seeming to have heard him. "But so many
colored newspapers have already failed. The few now appearing

are edited by men of much more education and literary training than yourself."

Douglass's buoyant optimism had faded. He sat with head
drooping as Garrison pounded home his point with several
more blows to the heart. Doubtless Douglass could learn to be
a good editor. His letters from England would have done
honor to a white man. And yet he was but nine years out of
slavery. (Garrison himself, a poor boy, had had very little formal education.)

Garrison continued with his calm certitude of knowing
everything better than anyone else in the world. "Most important," he said, "we can ill afford to lose a voice of such eloquence on the anti-slavery platform. All the details and drudg-
ery of editorship would leave you little time to speak."

Douglass had no choice but to yield to the arguments
of his friends, though some deep instinct raged against giving
up his dream. After all, Garrison managed to be both lecturer
and editor.

Garrison had need of his protégé for a new scheme. With
his genius for flying in the face of public opinion, Garrison had
decided on a Western tour with Douglass. Garrison was not
afraid of possible coolness from the practical Western abolitionists. He correctly guessed that curiosity to hear the flaming
fanatic and the former fugitive slave would fill all the halls.

The reaction of the Cleveland *Daily True Democrat* was
typical of their reception in Ohio. The paper found Garrison
"pleasant, clear, forcible and logical," but "Douglass is more
eloquent. He moves upon the passions of his audience and
handles with a master's skill the weapons of the orator." According to his friend William Wells Brown, Douglass was gaining
such a reputation as a speaker that young people used to creep
out of the house at night to hear him without the knowledge
of their stern Victorian parents.

Such applause was warming, but there was little chance
that it would swell Douglass's head. The insults and discrimi-

nation he had suffered on his westward journey confirmed all his reasons for wanting to start a paper. As he had sat in a corner hungry while the white men ate, Douglass remembered his warm welcome by lord mayors and parliamentary ministers.

Douglass felt increasingly remote from Garrison. The editor of *The Liberator*, ten years older than his companion, was looking pale and tired. Douglass sensed more and more that the black man must speak up for his rights with his own voice.

In Cleveland on September 17 they addressed an open-air meeting for several hours in a chill drizzle. When they got back to the house of their hosts, the kindly Smiths, Douglass noticed that Garrison looked flushed and sounded hoarse. By Monday he had collapsed.

Douglass tried to divert Garrison's mind by explaining why his original decision to publish a paper had been correct. When the doctor arrived, Garrison was near delirium.

Dr. Williams examined the patient and shook his head, muttering about "an intermittent fever with a tendency to typhoid." He prescribed an herb tea and complete rest. Douglass followed the instructions carefully, but Garrison tossed and babbled through the night.

In the morning Garrison woke up looking pale and weak but seeming more lucid. He was surprised that Douglass had not gone on to keep their engagements in Buffalo. Douglass assured him that he would not stir until Garrison improved.

"There can be no respite from this warfare," Garrison said sternly. "Mrs. Smith can nurse me."

Douglass followed orders but could not help worrying. A week later he was shocked to read in *The Liberator* that Garrison was still in danger. He hurried to confide his fears to an old friend, the Reverend Samuel J. May. May had come to Syracuse in 1845 to preside over the Unitarian church and local abolitionist activities.

May wrote Garrison that Douglass had left his side re-

The Reverend Samuel J. May

luctantly and only because he thought Garrison would follow him in a day or two. "His countenance fell, and his heart failed him, when he found me likewise in sad suspense about you."

A few days later Douglass was happy to read in *The Liberator* that Garrison was out of danger, though very weak. Now Douglass could devote his thoughts to his newspaper with a clear conscience. He was pained to think of the probable disapproval of his old friends. But he was now thirty years old. He knew he was too independent to follow forever another man's lead and think another man's thoughts. His English friends were only waiting for his word to send him the $2,100 needed to get started.

To keep friction with Boston at a minimum, Douglass decided to publish his paper in Rochester, New York, far from the circulation of *The Liberator* and *Standard*. This friendly and attractive city was situated on Lake Ontario near the terminus of the Erie Canal. Surrounded by rich farms and infant industries, Rochester was growing fast. Douglass remembered his warm reception by the Posts and the family of Samuel D. Porter, the bookseller.

Late in November there was a bustle of unusual activity in the basement of the A.M.E. Church in Rochester. The lamps flickered till after midnight as Frederick Douglass worked on the first issue of his newspaper with his new associates.

William C. Nell, named publisher of the new *North Star*, was later to become the first Negro historian of note. Nell, who came from Boston, was a staunch Garrisonian. Martin R. Delany, co-editor, had experience on the Pittsburgh *Mystery*. Freeborn and well educated, Delany had a brilliant, restless mind and a biting wit. Delany was to travel about, raising subscriptions while Douglass and Nell stayed in Rochester.

On Friday, December 3, 1847, Nell, Delany, and Douglass examined the first issue of *The North Star* in the printing offices of the Rochester *Democrat*. Across the masthead floated the slogan:

> Right is of no Sex—Truth is of no Color—God is the Father of us all, and we are all Brethren.

Delany and Nell looked excitedly over Douglass's shoulder. Together they read the brave words which were to be Douglass's battle cry for sixteen difficult but exhilarating years:

> We solemnly dedicate *The North Star* to the cause of our long oppressed and plundered fellow countrymen. May God bless the offering to your good! It shall fearlessly assert your rights, faithfully proclaim your wrongs, and

earnestly demand for you instant and evenhanded justice.
Giving no quarter to slavery at the South, it will hold no
truce with oppressors at the North. . . .

With his usual candor Douglass admitted that so far his
accomplishments had been more practical than literary. But
he assured his readers he would work hard to improve his style.
And he would gladly welcome contributions from more educated men. Through his efforts and the help of his subscribers:
"*The North Star* shall live."

Douglass expressed deep gratitude to his old Boston
friends. On the surface, all was smooth between Boston and
Rochester. Garrison joined in the chorus of praise for the new
paper and its editor. Favorable comments by leading abolitionists were printed in *The Liberator* and *Standard*.

Garrison, however, remained personally cool. He had
written his wife from Cleveland, complaining of Douglass's
lack of concern for his health. Douglass's conduct in starting
the paper, he told her irritably, had been "impulsive, inconsid-
erate and highly inconsistent with his decision in Boston."

Rochester, too, welcomed its new journal. The few sour
notes were not of local origin. The New York *Herald*, a penny
paper of strong prejudices, advised the citizens of Rochester to
throw the new press into the lake and chase the editor into
Canada. Rochester ignored this vulgar advice.

On a late January day in 1848 there was great excitement
along Alexander Street. The children were running up and
down the sidewalks and playing in the snowdrifts. Their parents indulged in much headshaking and tongue clicking behind the curtains.

At last came the muffled clop-clop of horses' hooves on
the packed snow, and the scrape of sleigh runners. Isaac Post
was driving, and at his side rode the imposing Negro who was
to be their new neighbor. The sleigh stopped in front of the
sturdy, comfortable brick house at Number 4. Frederick Doug-

Busy Rochester, seen from the west, in 1853. In the foreground, a steady stream of boats ply the Erie Canal. (From a lithograph)

lass handed out the small, round woman with the dark, stoic face, and four lively brown children, ranging from eight-and-a-half-year-old Rosetta to three-year-old Charles.

The children were delighted with the snow. Anna, however, seemed bundled into herself, and not only against the cold. Perhaps she had noticed that Rochester appeared to have an even smaller black community than Lynn.

Any thought that the neighbors may have had of protesting the presence of these black people faded at the sight of Douglass's dignified figure. There was something daunting, too, about the extreme reserve of Mrs. Douglass. Their immediate neighbors on each side were abolitionists; the others soon gained a reluctant admiration of the first black family they had ever known at close hand.

Anna's upbringing of her children and the efficient running of her household were aristocratic in their rigor. Rosetta had made a complete shirt for her father by the time she was ten. Later, finding they had few friends, Anna sent Rosetta and the older boys to the newspaper office to learn the printing trade. By the time they were in their teens they were helping set type and wrap the paper for mailing.

If the grown-ups were sometimes cool, the children quickly warmed to Douglass, who loved young people. Instead of scolding when they stole his apples, he made them feel ashamed. All of them remembered how on warm summer evenings he would stand in the window, singing to the accompaniment of the violin he had bought in England.

From the beginning of his stay in Rochester, Douglass's door opened to every well-known reformer and prominent European traveler who passed through the city. Even Southerners stopped by on their way to Niagara Falls to see if an ex-slave could really be writing so well. Anna, as Rosetta wrote of her later, was ill at ease in the "polite etiquette of the drawing room." She never felt comfortable with white people, and left the entertainment of distinguished guests to her husband.

Anna did not play hostess, but was cook and housekeeper. She expressed her pride in her husband by seeing that his shirts were always cleaned and starched by her own hand. She even mailed them to him while he was on lecture tours. She kept the house economically and immaculately. Her baking and cooking were legendary.

The only thing she could not learn to do to please her husband was read or write. A year after they came to Rochester, Douglass hired a teacher for her, but it was too late. She learned to read but one name—Frederick Douglass.

Douglass had need of all the friendship, support, and good wishes he could muster. The task he had undertaken would quickly have defeated a lesser man. Delany had little luck with his subscription tours. Most Northern Negroes could not afford two dollars a year. Delany, a man of varied interests, resigned within a year. He became the first Negro to enter Harvard Medical School.

With Delany gone, Douglass had to spend six months of the year on the road, as of old, lecturing and raising subscriptions. Once again he had to contend with the discomforts of frontier America. Once again he had to protest segregation on steamers and canal boats and in hotels and restaurants. Every year or so he came home to be nursed by Anna for his recurring bronchitis. Sometimes, he confided to his readers, he was too busy speaking to write his editorials. And sometimes his children were sick, or Anna had just had a baby—his beloved Annie, born in 1849.

A few months after its birth *The North Star* almost died. Reluctantly Douglass wrote of his difficulties to his English friend, Julia Griffiths. His funds were exhausted; he had had to mortgage his house for five hundred dollars to keep going.

Julia Griffiths was one of those strong-minded, energetic

Victorian women who were bored with the restricted oppor-
tunities open to their sex. With her sister Eliza she journeyed
into the unknown of America to become Douglass's right hand.
She ignored criticism of her unwomanly conduct and disre-
garded the slanderous abuse in the penny press resulting from
her friendship with a black man.

She and her sister strolled arm in arm with Douglass on
the streets of Rochester, on Broadway in New York, on the
deck of a steamer. With sublime unconcern they outfaced the
threats thickening the air. (These threats came not, Douglass
pointed out ironically, because he walked with them, but
because he walked with them as an equal, not a servant.)

Miss Griffiths took over the Female Anti-Slavery Society
and devoted its fund raising to supporting the newspaper. She
straightened out the muddle of Douglass's finances so that in
three years he was out of debt. She boosted the paper's circulation from two thousand to four thousand. She became
Douglass's English teacher. By the time she returned to England in 1855, Douglass's writing displayed the same vigor and
polish as his speaking.

Douglass also learned much from the better-educated Negroes whose contributions enlivened his paper. From New York
City Dr. James McCune Smith, a graduate of Glasgow University, sent in witty newsletters signed "Communipaw."
William Wells Brown wrote graceful, perceptive accounts of
his travels.

Douglass frequently lectured in Syracuse, where he made
friends with two important black leaders—both ministers. One
was the Reverend Jeremiah Wesley Loguen, a giant of a man,
a fugitive who had earned money to send himself to Oneida
Institute. The other was the Reverend Samuel Ringgold Ward,
a cousin and classmate of Garnet's from New York City. Both
men wrote for *The North Star*.

No other black leader ever impressed Douglass as did
Ward. His appearance was striking—Wendell Phillips said
he was so black that when he closed his eyes one could not see

Frederick Douglass in the late 1840s

him. His eloquence was rated by Douglass as superior to his own. The quiet, majestic Ward, with his breadth of learning, spoke with a classic purity and logic that served as a model for the more emotional and impetuous Douglass.

Douglass's work on the paper drew him closer not only to black leaders but to all his people. Every week now, without the support of the Garrisonians, he had to grapple personally and editorially with all those problems besetting the "nominally free" Negroes of the North. Among them were separate schools, separate churches, job discrimination, discrimination in public accommodations.

Douglass had to consider which was more desirable for

his people—separate institutions or the far-off, often seemingly unattainable, goal of integration. Soon after Douglass became an editor, Dr. James McCune Smith wrote the New York State abolitionist Gerrit Smith that Douglass was "like one newly born among us." For the first time, he seemed to "become a colored man."

Soon Douglass was raising his voice in indignation over all the wrongs to his people. Of course he denounced slavery, but also the ruffians who would throw a black man off a Northern train, whether a poor lame workingman or his friend Garnet. He pointed out the existence of plundering mobs in the North. With biting humor he described his many brushes with prejudice in his travels. He warned black laborers that they were being forced out of their old jobs by immigrants and must "learn trades or starve."

None of these struggles came closer to Douglass's heart than the attempt to secure integrated education for black children. He discovered that his own children had to walk across the city to a segregated school in the damp, crowded, dingy basement under Zion Church. Douglass refused to send them to a segregated school. After eight years of agitation, aided by a few white friends like the Porters, Douglass finally won desegregation of the Rochester schools in 1857.

But meanwhile the Douglass children had to learn to read, write, and spell. In August 1848 Douglass was delighted to find that Seward Seminary, run by a reputed abolitionist, Miss Tracy, would accept Rosetta.

Douglass was away speaking in Cleveland when the term opened a month later. He could scarcely wait to get back and hear of Rosetta's first days in a really good school. He did not notice the veiled pain in her eyes as she ran to his arms upon his return.

"Well, my daughter, how do you get on at the seminary?" he asked.

"I get along pretty well, but father, Miss Tracy does not

allow me to go into the room with the other scholars because I am colored."

"Stung to the heart's core," Douglass hurried to the seminary and insisted on seeing Miss Tracy at once. Averting her eyes, that lady paced the floor of her office, knotting and unknotting her handkerchief.

"You see," she appealed to him, "the board of trustees hadn't known of my decision to accept your daughter. They were very much opposed; I couldn't ignore their advice when it is they who support my school."

"But you did accept my daughter; and then you treat her like a common criminal, subjecting her to solitary confinement. I cannot conceive of such cruelty to an unoffending little girl."

"Of course, you know my feelings on the slavery question," said Miss Tracy, who had sat down at her desk and was studying a blown glass paperweight. "I think if we teach your daughter separately for a term or two, and she proves amenable, this prejudice may yet be overcome."

"I cannot consent to such an arrangement. It would humiliate my daughter both in her own eyes and those of the other children. I'm afraid Mrs. Douglass will agree with me that we must at once withdraw our daughter from Seward Seminary,—unless you are willing to submit the question to the young ladies themselves."

"Well," said Miss Tracy doubtfully, "there can be no harm in that." She rang a large bronze bell.

As each child entered, she approached Miss Tracy's desk and curtsied. Then she was asked if she had any objection to receiving Rosetta Douglass into the school. She must be sure she had not the slightest dislike to the idea. But despite the discouraging form of the question, each girl was glad to vote in favor of admitting the daughter of Frederick Douglass.

Miss Tracy seemed especially astonished when this answer came from the school's most delicate blonde.

"Did you mean to vote so? Are you *accustomed* to black

persons?" asked the principal. The girl looked puzzled, then lined up beside her friends. Miss Tracy still seemed dissatisfied.

"But if we accept her as equal among us, by whom may she sit?" she asked.

"By me, by me," chorused several young voices.

"Well, you shall submit the question to your parents and, if one objects, she must remain apart."

Douglass went home, supposing victory was won. But at noon next day Rosetta came home in tears with her books, pens, and papers. One parent, Horatio B. Warner of the Rochester *Courier*, had refused permission for his daughter to attend school with her. In the winter term of 1849 Douglass was able to place Rosetta at an equally good school in Albany.

With Rosetta happy, Douglass wrote an open letter to Warner. After recounting the whole story, Douglass explained his reasons for making it public:

> If this were a private affair, only affecting myself and family, I should possibly allow it to pass without attracting public attention to it; but such is not the case. It is a deliberate attempt to degrade and injure a large class of persons, whose rights and feelings have been the common sport of yourself, and such persons as yourself, for ages, and I think it unwise to allow you to do so with impunity. Thank God, oppressed and plundered as we are and have been, we are not without help. We have a press, open and free, and have ample means by which we are able to proclaim our wrongs as a people, and your own infamy, and that proclamation shall be as complete as the means in my power can make it.

Frederick Douglass never better expressed his reasons for starting *The North Star* against the advice of his Garrisonian friends. Month after month and year after year his pen spoke out with the same proud vigor as his voice. It was small wonder that he became known as the "Tribune of His People."

11 politics and runaways

The measures maturing at Washington are not only intended to fasten the chains of slavery more firmly upon the limbs of the slave, and to make the North less secure for the fugitive, but they strike a fatal blow at the liberty of every colored man in the North.

Frederick Douglass

The mobs of New York City were in a nasty mood in May 1850. A new spirit of strain and tension was rising in the land on the heels of the Mexican War. At last the boundaries of the nation had been pushed to the Pacific. Would the vast new stretches of fertile prairies and towering mountain peaks be controlled by the North or the South, by free states or slave states?

Southern firebrands like Robert Toombs called for disunion if the North sought to drive slavery from the rich lands of the West. Northern anti-slavery senators like William Seward, as well as abolitionists, spoke out against any more concessions to the Slave Power.

In this atmosphere of doubt and danger, the American Anti-Slavery Society was holding its annual meeting at the Broadway Tabernacle. The businessmen of New York were worried. Times were good. If this disunion talk went on, the bottom would drop out of the cotton market. Some of the newspapers were openly inciting to riot. James Gordon Bennett of the *Herald* led the way, urging New Yorkers to:

> go on Tuesday morning to the Tabernacle and there look at the black and white brethren and sisters, fraternizing and slobbering over each other, speaking, singing, blaspheming and cursing the Constitution and the Union,

The Reverend Samuel Ringgold Ward

and then say whether these things shall go forth to the
South and the world as the feeling of the great city of New
York.

The city's always explosive mixture of immigrant laborers,
Four Points ruffians, idlers, gamblers, and seamen at liberty
answered the call. On May 8 they joined the several hundred
abolitionists gathered at the Broadway Tabernacle.

Francis Jackson, the same Boston gentleman who had
presided at the *Telegraph* protest, was in the chair. Next to
him on the platform were Phillips, Garrison, Unitarian min-

ister the Reverend Dr. William H. Furness, Samuel Ringgold Ward, and Douglass.

Garrison was explaining that abolitionists were the only
true Christians in America. "A belief in Jesus is no proof of
goodness," he said in his quiet way of announcing outrageous
truths.

This shot set off a louder hissing, and a figure popped up
in the gallery. It was Captain Isaiah Rynders, a professional
gambler, a Tammany ward heeler and a man tougher than the
toughest members of his gang. He had suddenly "got religion":

"Are you aware that the slaves in the South have their
prayer meetings in honor of Christ?"

Garrison answered fearlessly, shockingly, "Not in a slaveholding Jesus. But in a Jesus that strikes off chains!"

Rynders had his signal; he stampeded down the aisles
from the gallery with his bloodhounds at heel. A tremor passed
through the audience, but no one moved.

Rynders bounded to the platform to wave his fist under
Garrison's nose. Young Thomas Kane leaped from a box to
shake *his* fist in Rynder's face. "If he touches Mr. Garrison,
I'll *kill* him," he cried.

Garrison merely said gently to the blustery red face, "We
go on the principle of hearing everybody. I will keep order and
you shall be heard."

Rynders beckoned to one of his seediest-looking followers
—"Professor" Grant—while the rest of the pack settled un-
easily into the first rows. Grant "vociferated and harangued"
for some time on the theme that blacks were not men but a
tribe of monkeys. The audience, growing weary of the venom,
began to call for Frederick Douglass to answer the crude charges
made against his race.

Douglass rose slowly, majestically. Never had he looked
more like an African king. His voice boomed out, "The gentleman who has just spoken has undertaken to prove that blacks
are not human beings. He has examined our whole confor-
mation. I cannot follow him in his argument. I will assist him

in it, however." Turning to Rynders, "I offer myself for your examination. Am I a man?"

Rynders snapped back, "You are not a black man; you are only half a *nigger*."

"Then I am half-brother to Captain Rynders."

Then Douglass turned to the audience with an eloquent plea for the just claims of his race. He ended:

> We were born here. We are not dying out and we mean to stay here. We made the clothes you have on, the sugar you put into your tea. We would do more if allowed.

"Yes," shouted one of Rynders's men, "You would cut our throats for us."

"No," answered Douglass, "but we would cut your hair for you. . . . And now, since I am not black enough to satisfy Captain Rynders, I am happy to present a friend of mine who is."

As the Reverend Samuel Ringgold Ward came forward, Rynders stood openmouthed and said, "Well, this is the original nigger."

Ward replied in his most urbane voice, "I've heard of the magnanimity of Captain Rynders, but the half has not been told me."

Ward, speaking that day with his highest blending of passion and logic, brought down the house. "What a grand triumph of intelligence over brute force" these two black men demonstrated, Dr. Furness wrote later.

As Douglass journeyed up the Hudson on the steamer *Alida*, he felt as if he were traveling backward. In the end, Rynders had succeeded in breaking up the convention. Worst of all, the city of New York had not raised a finger to protect the delegates. All their gains of the last decade seemed to shrink and retreat before the new aggressiveness of the pro-slavery forces.

In the halls of Congress, Henry Clay, the Great Compromiser, was working on one last agreement to satisfy North and South and cement the Union more firmly. For his love of the Union, even Daniel Webster was willing to accept a stronger, more distasteful fugitive slave law in exchange for California as a free state and the end of the slave trade in the District of Columbia.

When Douglass reached home, Anna told him that word had come from Peterboro for him to visit as soon as he was able. Gerrit Smith, the rich, eccentric owner of that vast estate, was a leader of the Liberty party. Ever since Douglass had come to Rochester, Smith had been carrying on a friendly debate with him.

Smith combined a deep, simple Methodist faith with a dislike for dogmatic religion. He acted out his religion by his never-failing generosity. "God," he would say, "gave me money to give away." Among his many charities was aid—both money and shelter—to fugitive slaves. In this work he grew close to Douglass and would send contributions to *The North Star*.

As the carriage bearing Douglass rolled up to the front door of Smith's many-roomed mansion, Douglass wondered whom he would meet under the hospitable millionaire's roof. Douglass had shared Smith's long table with men and women of every religion, abolitionists and Northern "dough-face" (pro-Southern) politicians, fugitive slaves and Southern slaveholders. All were equally welcome—and at the same time.

Douglass was delighted to see a familiar face among a group of three ladies talking on the lawn. Elizabeth Cady Stanton, a cousin of Smith, ran to meet him with a joyous laugh, her plump and pretty face alight. She had converted Douglass to the cause of woman's rights in Boston when her husband, Henry B. Stanton, was a young lawyer practicing there. Mrs. Stanton now lived in nearby Seneca Falls. Douglass often met her at anti-slavery or woman's rights meetings.

The white-haired, white-bearded Smith greeted Douglass warmly; he turned around to present the other two ladies,

Gerrit Smith

cousins of his from the Deep South. But they had disappeared.
For the whole two weeks that Douglass remained at Peterboro,
the two ladies insisted on remaining in their apartment and
taking their meals there.

Mrs. Stanton suspected that they may later have regretted
their decision. The late spring weather remained so clear and
warm that she, Gerrit Smith, and Douglass spent much of
their time talking on the lawn. The talk was serious, but at
the end of each day, in the soft and fragrant twilight, Douglass
would tell funny stories of his adventures on the road or sing
songs to guitar accompaniment under the ladies' window.

When Douglass told Smith and Mrs. Stanton about the

mobs attacking the convention in New York, it dramatized the forces that were pushing the Fugitive Slave Act through Congress. If this law should actually be passed, the Underground Railroad, which they all supported, would become more vital than ever.

In September 1850 the worst happened. The Fugitive Slave Act was adopted by Congress, along with the other provisions of the Compromise of 1850. Now any Negro might be accused of being a fugitive and be returned to slavery on a simple affidavit of a man claiming to be his owner. Federal judges, commissioners, and marshals were to enforce the act; there would be no trial by jury.

A shock of alarm passed among the black people of the North. Business on the Underground Railroad was suddenly booming. But now it was not only fugitive slaves who used the barns and houses of white and black "station masters and conductors." Whole settlements disappeared overnight. One Baptist church in Rochester lost all but two members.

Black leaders joined the exodus. Henry Highland Garnet set off on a three-year tour of England and the Continent. William Wells Brown, already abroad, decided to stay longer. Then Ward left for Canada and England, never to return. "Who," groaned Douglass when he heard it, "is left?"

In this atmosphere of crisis and panic, Douglass stood firm. He had sworn on returning home free from England that, rather than enjoy honor and peace abroad, he would suffer with his brethren in chains. He would "struggle in their ranks for that emancipation which shall yet be achieved by the power of truth and principle." Now he redeemed his promise.

Fortunately, he had some new allies. The Fugitive Slave Act had shocked even men of conservative temperament. They might care nothing for the Negro, free or slave. But they did not like to see a man of any color dragged off to involuntary servitude without his constitutional right to a trial by jury.

As the bill became law, Douglass was addressing a meeting of protest in Corinthian Hall, Rochester. Douglass stood before his friends and neighbors as a man whose own life was in danger. Dramatically he cried, "Is there a man here who says he has a right to sell his brother?"

From the rear a voice piped up, "I do."

"Then turn your face to the wall," said Douglass, pointing at the man scornfully.

Among the friends listening who shuddered was young Susan B. Anthony, daughter of the Quaker abolitionists, Asa and Hulda Anthony. The towering figure before her, threatened by an unjust law, was the same man whose family the Anthonys so often entertained on a Sunday. When the Anthony wagon brought them out to the farm, the young Douglasses would dash off across the fields for a romp. Douglass would then discuss abolition and temperance with the older Anthonys.

Miss Anthony had returned a year ago from teaching in Canajoharie, New York, to run her parents' farm. She had already discovered a talent for speaking after her address to the Local Daughters of Temperance. In this moment of peril for her friend, Miss Anthony dedicated herself on the spot to the cause of abolition.

Douglass, the Anthonys, the Porters, the Posts, and all the abolitionists of Rochester threw their energies more and more into the work of the Underground Railroad. Rochester was one of the last stops in New York before the freedom of Canada.

Douglass became stationmaster for the city and moved into a larger house on South Avenue in suburban Pinnacle Hills. Hidden in the woods and reached only by an Indian path, his new house was safer for both the Douglasses and the increasing number of fugitives they sheltered.

Sometimes Horace McGuire, one of Douglass's white apprentices, would find runaways sitting on the steps of the newspaper office when he arrived to open it at 6:30 A.M. Then Douglass would spirit them away to E. C. Williams's sail loft,

local abolitionist Dr. Clark's quiet home, or the farmhouses
and barns of the Anthonys and Posts.

Often Douglass would go out into the street and pass the
hat to raise money for food and fares. *The North Star* and
Frederick Douglass' Paper (as the *Star* was later known) were
full of appeals for funds. Though fugitives were returned South
from other cities and states, none was ever retaken in Rochester,
New York.

In September 1851 Douglass was in bed with one of his
recurring attacks of bronchitis. Anna hurried in, her usually
inexpressive face agitated. Her husband must see three men
who waited downstairs. Forgetting his fever, Douglass pulled
on his dressing gown and walked over to the desk.

The three young black men who were shown in were somehow different from the shivering, confused refugees that Douglass so often sheltered. They had the resolute look of men quite
ready to defend themselves. The leader, a slim, clear-eyed
young man, walked over and laid a rifle on the desk.

"Mr. Douglass, this gun has killed a man. Do you wish to
help a murderer escape to Canada?"

"Are you William Parker? Your story has just come over
the wires. Keep your gun; you may need it. To me you are no
murderer but a defender of the just rights of man." Douglass
held out his hand, which the other gripped fervently. "I regret
that my illness hampers me in aiding you, but I have friends."
He scribbled a note to Samuel Porter under his code name of
reversed initials.

> There are three men now at my house who are in
> great peril. I am unwell, I need your advice. Please come
> at once. D. F.

Douglass consulted with Porter and Julia Griffiths. It was
agreed that Miss Griffiths should arrange their passage to Canada while Porter secured the money.

That evening, weak as he was, Douglass drove the three

fugitives to the boat landing in Samuel Porter's wagon. As Parker started aboard, he turned to Douglass and handed him the fatal gun.

The Christiana tragedy, in which Parker had been involved, was to make headlines throughout the country. Parker, a free Negro farmer of Lancaster County, Pennsylvania, frequently hid fugitives who crossed the border from Maryland. Two days before, a slaveholder named Gorsuch, his son, and several United States marshals had attacked his house on suspicion he was harboring one of Gorsuch's slaves.

Parker and his friends had fired back at the raiding party; their shots had killed Gorsuch, fatally wounded his son, and also grazed two of the marshals. Then Parker and his two aides had melted into the cornfields and made their way to Rochester.

As more and more fugitives passed through his house, Douglass began to feel remote from the Boston abolitionists. It seemed to him that their high, narrow principles were out of touch with the heart beat of America and the great sources of power. Disunion, which they preached, would only leave the slaves at the mercy of the slaveholders. Attacking all religion was wrong and foolish—many Northern churches had split with the Southern branch because the Northerners were anti-slavery in sympathy.

These new ideas finally brought Douglass to an important decision that had been a long time in the making. He agreed with Gerrit Smith that the real spirit of the Constitution was opposed to slavery. He accepted Smith's offer to merge the *Liberty Party Paper* with *The North Star* and become editor of both under the new name of *Frederick Douglass' Paper*.

Douglass set off for the annual meeting of the American Anti-Slavery Society with misgivings. He knew Garrison was not a man tolerant of those who differed from his views. The coolness with which Garrison greeted him emphasized how far apart they had already grown. Remond hardly spoke to him, jealousy having finally killed their friendship. Yet, would not

Douglass himself have remained in a secondary position if he had never left the protective shadow of Garrison and Boston to strike out on his own?

Douglass had decided to make an "open and manly" confession of his new views before the convention. When he stood up, he hesitated and stuttered more than at any time since his debut ten years before:

> I have concluded that the Constitution might be consistent in the details with the noble purpose avowed in its preamble. My opinions have also changed materially in relation to the duty of political action. In short, I would no longer oppose it.

Garrison, in the chair, turned white, as if stunned by an electric charge. "There is roguery somewhere!" he cried.

A caricature, more gentle than most, of a Woman's Rights Convention, *with hooting spectators in the gallery (From* Harper's Weekly)

These were bitter words to Douglass. Try as he would, he could not shake them from his mind. Garrison was like a domineering father whose son could not break away from him and grow up except by an open act of rebellion. With the passing of years and the hardening of his views, Garrison had become convinced that his way was the only way to fight slavery. He thought those who opposed him were less virtuous than he. Given Douglass's more flexible mind, he would probably have quarreled with Garrison sooner or later, anyway.

For a while, however, it seemed as if the incident might lead to nothing worse than still greater coolness between Rochester and Boston. Douglass returned to his office and changed the name of his paper, announcing his new views in an editorial. He adopted a motto suggested by Gerrit Smith, "All Rights for All," for *Frederick Douglass' Paper*. Douglass worked harder and longer than ever to live up to that motto.

Douglass had long been appreciative of the great contribution of women to the anti-slavery movement. When his friend Elizabeth Cady Stanton had called the first Woman's Rights Convention at Seneca Falls, he had been one of the few men courageous enough to attend. The ridicule heaped on all who went to these early conventions did not disturb one who had been called far nastier names than an "Aunt Nancy man."

When Mrs. Stanton had proposed a resolution that women be given the vote, even most of the women thought it too radical. But Douglass calmly seconded it. Soon Susan B. Anthony met Mrs. Stanton and began a lifelong partnership for woman's rights. Miss Anthony told her friends to look for announcements of meetings in *Douglass' Paper*.

Other reforms which Douglass supported were temperance, the abolition of capital punishment, and universal education "for every poor man from Maine to Texas."

Most of all, however, Douglass threw himself into the fight to raise the position of the Northern Negro. His voice rose loud and clear as he joined men like McCune Smith,

Pennington, Charles Reason, Charles B. Ray, the Langston brothers, George and John B. Vashon, and George T. Downing at every convention called by the free Negroes of the North.

Douglass tried to ignore the criticism of him that began to appear in the Garrisonian press and at Garrisonian conventions. He wrote that he wished "to maintain silence under whatever Mr. Garrison may say. I stand in relation to him something like that of a child to a parent."

Garrison and his followers soon made Douglass's silence all but impossible. In the winter of 1852-53 the smoldering quarrel burst into the open. When Garrison indiscreetly hinted at scandal in Douglass's relation to Miss Griffiths, the fat was in the fire. Douglass began trading charge for charge.

Did the Fosters and Henry Wright find him a traitor to Garrison? Douglass accused them of "religious infidelity." When William Nell left Rochester, calling his former friend "unkind, ungenerous and ungrateful," Douglass in turn called Nell "a contemptible tool" and "an enemy of the colored people." Robert Purvis, the wealthy, almost-white son of a Southern merchant, he accused of having "blood-stained riches." Remond he regarded as his bitterest enemy.

Like all such angry name-calling, the controversy between Douglass and the Garrisonians generated much heat and little light. It did not help either side and undoubtedly weakened the abolitionist movement.

Yet there was one charge Douglass hurled against Garrison himself which underscored the limitations of many white abolitionists in understanding the aims of the black man. Garrison had written:

> . . . the Anti-Slavery cause both religiously and politically, has transcended the ability of the sufferers from American slavery and prejudice, *as a class*, to keep pace with it, or to perceive what are its demands, or to understand the philosophy of its operations.

Douglass had suffered too long from the patronizing attitude which implied that the abolitionist movement was too good for the slave and the free Negro it was supposed to help. His reply was indignant:

> Who will doubt, hereafter, the natural inferiority of the *Negro*, when the great champion of the Negroes' rights, thus broadly concedes all that is claimed respecting the Negro's inferiority by the bitterest despisers of the Negro race?

His answers, of course, had no effect on the Garrisonians. Garrison himself was an especially passionate enemy who rarely forgave a slight. He was never really reconciled to Douglass.

But in later years, when the smoke of battle had cleared and emancipation had been attained, Douglass worked side by side again with Wendell Phillips, Parker Pillsbury, and others to gain citizenship and the vote for his people. He also gave full credit to the pioneer work of Garrison and his central importance in the great fight.

The black abolitionists who followed Garrison had joined in condemning Douglass. However, a large majority of the black community supported him, denouncing Garrison's "vile crusade" against him. With such backing, Douglass went forth lonelier, sadder perhaps, but unafraid to fight the battles of the black man on every front.

12 john brown goes marching

To have been acquainted with John Brown, shared his counsels, enjoyed his confidence, and sympathized with the great objects of his life and death, I esteem as among the highest privileges of my life.

Frederick Douglass

In April 1859 Horace McGuire, Douglass's white apprentice, was alone in the newspaper office. The door opened suddenly and he saw framed in it a strange white man with grizzled hair and beard, hollow cheeks, and eyes that pierced whatever they rested on.

"I will wait for Mr. Douglass here," he announced in a matter-of-fact voice that discouraged contradiction.

McGuire was surprised. His employer was so often away on speaking tours that even his best friends did not always know when he was in town. McGuire tried to concentrate on setting his type, but was constantly aware of the old man in his battered hat and worn coat, restlessly pacing back and forth.

When Douglass came, he rushed up to the man, flung his strong arms around the thin, sinewy shoulders, and said with great warmth, "So you've come, my old friend."

"Yes, my dear Douglass, my plans are almost set, and you shall be the first to hear of them. I am on my way to Peterboro." The old man's voice was as sharp and clear as a knife stroke.

"But first you must see Green," said Douglass. "Surely you remember him from last year—one of my fugitives, a man of unusual character though he's suffered much."

"All such fugitives are dear to me as brothers." There was something profoundly thrilling about the way the old man uttered these words. "You and he shall meet me before long."

Douglass felt the flame of the other man's single-minded intensity once more. Only John Brown, of all the whites he knew, could have stated with utter sincerity that every runaway slave was his brother in the deepest, truest sense.

Douglass had been shaken by Brown's power since he met him in 1848. At the urging of some of his black friends, he had looked up Brown while lecturing in Springfield, Massachusetts, where Brown then kept a store. "You must meet the only white man who really understands slavery," the fiery Garnet had whispered.

Sometimes that whole first meeting seemed to Douglass like a dream, except that the memory of it was still so sharp. First there had been the prosperous store of Perkins and Brown, wool merchants, and then, in sharp contrast, the smallest, plainest house on an unfashionable street, where Douglass had been invited to dine.

Indelibly impressed on Douglass's mind had been the picture of Brown seated at the head of the unpainted, unvarnished table that provided the only furniture of the bare main room within. Douglass thought him "a figure straight and symmetrical as a mountain pine."

Brown had blessed the bread with a biblical simplicity. His many sons and daughters, his wife, and Douglass bowed their heads in reverence. The simple, hearty meal of beef soup, cabbage, and potatoes reflected Brown's background as an Ohio pioneer rather than his current life as a city merchant.

When the meal was finished, Brown turned to Douglass. He revealed his great plans, hesitantly at first, then with greater fierceness.

"Douglass, neither moral suasion nor political action can liberate a single slave. Slavery is a sin so monstrous that the slaveholder has forfeited his right to live. Therefore, I say a slave has a right to gain his freedom in any way he is able. A system based on blood and terror must perish in blood and terror."

Frederick Douglass felt a tremor in his very soul. These

John Brown in 1848

were the words of Walker and Garnet, of Denmark Vesey and Nat Turner, and of every slave who, like Douglass, had ever planned to break for freedom.

Then Brown unrolled a map of the Allegheny Mountains, which stretched from the New York border deep into the South.

"God has given the strength of the hills to freedom," said Brown. "They are full of forts where one man for defense will be equal to a hundred for attack."

Brown intended to take twenty-five picked men, arm them, and post them on a line of twenty-five miles in those mountains. Swooping down from these hills, his men could "run off" slaves from the fields below.

Douglass fought against the spell of Brown's personality. What would the bands live on?

On the land, answered Brown. Slavery was a state of war.

Wouldn't the slaveholders simply sell their slaves farther south?

Maybe at first, admitted Brown, but think what a victory

it would be if slavery could be driven out of even one county.

But the bloodhounds?

"We should whip them!"

"And if you should be cut off?"

"We would cut our way out. I should but be killed at worst, and I have no better use for my life than to lay it down to destroy slavery."

Brown denied that the slaveholders would ever have their proud hearts softened by moral persuasion. He knew them too well. So he lived simply and saved his money for the great day.

By the time he left, Douglass was profoundly shaken. Memories he had tried to suppress flooded back. Again he saw Captain Anthony beating Aunt Esther, Colonel Lloyd in his pride, Thomas Auld ordering him to be broken by Edward Covey. What, to such people, were Garrison's and Phillips's calls to conscience?

The seed that Brown had planted took a long time to grow, but sometimes it would send up shoots. Less than a year later Douglass said openly to a Faneuil Hall audience:

> When I consider . . . the history of the American people,—how they bared their bosoms to the storm of British artillery, in order to resist a simple three-penny tax, and to assert their independence of the mother country—I should welcome the intelligence tomorrow, should it come, that the slaves had risen in the South, and that the sable arms which had been engaged in beautifying and adorning the South were engaged in spreading death and devastation there.

More and more during the perilous 1850s Douglass would remember the words of John Brown and his simple no-quarter solution to the slavery problem. More and more, North and South eyed each other across their dividing line as enemies.

The national tension was reflected in the delicate position of the Northern Negro. By 1859 emancipation for the slaves and more rights for free Negroes seemed further away than they had ten years earlier.

Douglass's paper was failing for lack of support. His weekly had to become a *Monthly*. The Liberty party and its successor, the Radical Abolitionist party, never commanded more than a small percentage of the electorate despite the devoted efforts of Douglass and Gerrit Smith.

Many of Douglass's friends, like Garnet and Delany, began to favor emigration of all Negroes to Africa or South America. Douglass fought back against "the lying assumption that white and black people can never live in the same land on terms of equality." But sometimes, in his discouragement, he wondered.

The Kansas-Nebraska Act of 1854 had set a match to the smoldering antagonisms between North and South. This law stated that the settlers should decide for themselves whether the new territories of Kansas and Nebraska should become slave or free states. Senator Stephen A. Douglas, the adroit author of this idea of "squatter sovereignty," thought it would please everyone.

Instead the North was appalled. This law broke forever the Missouri Compromise of 1820, which banned slavery north of 36° 30' latitude. All over the North it was denounced, and not by abolitionists alone. In July a group of anti-slavery men and Free Soilers met in Jackson, Michigan, to found a new party —the Republican—opposed to any more extension of slavery.

North and South, rich men put up the money to help homesteaders from their section settle in Kansas and dominate its politics. Most settlers wanted only the new, rich, cheap land, but they packed their rifles. They were joined by the lawless who flock to any frontier, spoiling for a fight. Inevitably guerrilla war broke out, and John Brown turned up right in the middle of it with two of his sons.

In the spring of 1856 the Missouri men looted and burned the free-state capital of Lawrence, Kansas. Now Brown's blinding hatred of slavery found a target. One midnight in May 1856 he and his band dragged five proslavery men from their beds near Pottawatomie Creek and ruthlessly slaughtered them.

Far from being shocked by Brown's actions, a group of prominent abolitionists, mostly from Boston, financed his movements in Kansas and promised future support for his great plan, revealed long ago to Douglass. These men were the young, ardent Unitarian minister, Thomas Wentworth Higginson, already famous for his unsuccessful attempt to prevent the return of the fugitive Anthony Burns; the even younger Franklin Sanborn, excited by the secret plots and meetings; the ever-generous Gerrit Smith; the equally rich George L. Stearns; the scholarly abolitionist minister Theodore Parker; and the old freedom fighter and humanitarian Samuel Gridley Howe.

By the end of 1857 Kansas was quiet. The settlers had rejected a proslavery constitution. Not long after, in February 1858, neighbors who were close enough to the Douglass home on South Avenue to glimpse it through the trees noticed strange goings and comings. Young Fred and Charles rushed back and forth to the post office with letters to or from N. Hawkins. These letters were addressed to Peterboro and Boston. In one window the candles burned most of the night. By their light John Brown was composing a strange constitution for the mountain republic which he hoped to set up at last.

Perhaps the strangest sight of all was that of Brown sitting on a snowy hillside, on a rock, with little Annie on his knee, bundled against the cold. Opposite him sat the other children, for whom he built towers of blocks or traced designs of fortifications in the snow. Fugitive Shields "The Emperor" Green often sat near them, as fascinated as the children. This much-abused man, whose speech was as broken as his body, had accomplished the unbelievable feat of escaping North from Charleston, South Carolina.

Brown had intended to go ahead with his plan that year, when disaster struck. A disgruntled associate of Brown from

Kansas, Hugh Forbes, told a group of anti-slavery senators
about the plot. The senators were furious. They complained to
Brown's supporters. Quickly the committee wrote Brown—Go
back to Kansas; wait till the excitement dies down; next spring
we will raise more money for you.

That was why Brown had turned up at the newspaper
office in the spring of 1859. Right in the presence of Horace
McGuire he told Douglass the time was ripe. How exciting
his words sounded to the deskbound apprentice, who remembered them all his life.

From then on Brown's preparations grew more intense.
He collected money and rifles. He raised a small army of sixteen white men and four runaway slaves.

In August 1859 Brown wrote Douglass to meet him at an
old quarry near Chambersburg, Pennsylvania, bringing money
and Shields Green. When Douglass and Green reached the
quarry they peered over the rim, and at first saw no one. Finally
they barely made out an old man with a fishing pole in a battered hat and suit as gray as the quarry stone. His wary look
changed to a smile as he motioned them to his side. His "Secretary of War," Kagi, then appeared from behind a rock. They
all sat down side by side on the giant stone steps.

"This is the eleventh hour, my friend. We have the chance
to strike a real blow at the vitals of the slave system." Brown's
voice whipped against the walls of rock and rebounded.

Douglass sat up very straight. His face had the look of
deeply etched sorrow that middle age and perpetual crisis were
engraving there.

"The old plan of running off slaves to the mountains is too
slow, too long. We must move faster; I mean to attack the
government arsenal at Harper's Ferry. The place is impregna-
ble, and when I am in control there, the slaves will rise as if at
the call of a trumpet!"

To Douglass it must have seemed as if his friend were
pushing a knife through his heart, calmly smiling all the time.
"My dear old friend, this is madness. You would be walking

into a trap. They will surround you and blast or starve you out."

"I suppose we could cut our way out if we had to, but we won't. I shall take the best men of the neighborhood as my hostages."

"If you attack and seize government property, they will blow you up, and your hostages, too, if they must. Slow but sure is better in the long run than vain heroics."

All that day and most of the next the two men argued their opposing views in friendly, respectful tones. But neither would budge. As the afternoon shadows lengthened on Sunday, Douglass shook his head. "I see, my friend, that you have decided to walk into this death trap," he said. "I would gladly aid the slaves in any way possible, with my very breath, if need be, but this mad plan will not help them at all. And your brave men will lay down their lives for nothing."

Green, who had watched and listened the whole time, looked at Brown with an unblinking gaze. Brown threw his arms around Douglass. His face lit up, but Douglass looked sadder than ever.

"Come with me, Douglass; I will defend you with my life; I want you for a special purpose. When I strike, the bees will begin to swarm, and I shall want you to help hive them."

"Alas, I must go to my work as you to yours." Douglass turned to Green. "You are a free man; stay with him or go with me, as you will."

The fugitive moved closer to Brown. "I b'leve I'll go wid de ole man."

So Frederick Douglass walked away from John Brown for the last time.

On the evening of October 19 Douglass was delivering a lecture to a full house in National Hall, Philadelphia. The lecture was entitled "Self-Made Men," and he was to deliver it many times in his life. It described those who, like himself, had risen to fame "from the depths of poverty" through "patient, enduring, honest, unremitting work."

In back of him on the platform he heard some agitated

murmurs. But Douglass ignored them and finished his talk to enthusiastic applause. As soon as he stepped off the platform a friend grasped his wrist.

"Yesterday John Brown attacked the government arsenal at Harper's Ferry," the friend told Douglass. "He barricaded himself in the engine house with a few runaway slaves, some hostages, and a small company of men."

The circle of friendly faces around Douglass could not miss the look of consternation that crossed his face. One of his best friends, Franklin Turner, urged him to fly at once.

"Let's not panic," said Douglass, holding his voice steady. "Wait to see what the morning brings."

The next day Douglass waited in the house of Thomas Dorsey while the news grew worse each hour. Brown and a few of his men were facing a body of Virginia militia led by Col. Robert E. Lee. The late afternoon paper announced that Lee and his men had broken into the engine house and captured the survivors. They found a critically wounded Brown, looking calmly at the body of his dead son while he held the hand of another son, who was dying.

Governor Wise of Virginia hurried to visit him on his stretcher. He told the press: "They are themselves mistaken who take him to be a madman. . . . He is a man of clear head, of fortitude and simple ingenuousness."

A warning from a friendly telegraph operator, John Hurn, finally sent Douglass north to New York and over the river to spend the night in Hoboken, New Jersey. Meanwhile, Hurn held a wire to the sheriff of Philadelphia in his pocket for three hours.

Douglass read in the morning *Herald* the reason for Hurn's warning. Brown's letters had implicated him and Gerrit Smith, along with members of the Boston committee. Douglass and Smith were to be the subject of a requisition upon Governor Morgan of New York to be delivered to the State of Virginia as accessories before the fact to the crime of murder.

New York, ever sensitive to Southern trade winds, was reflecting a growing hysteria in that section about Brown's raid. The phantom threat of a slave insurrection, so often raised, had been so close to reality! The South cried out for new, stiffer laws—against free Negroes, against free speech.

In this superheated atmosphere Douglass's friends put him on the Erie Railroad in Paterson under cover of night. At his request they wired B. F. Blackall at the Rochester telegraph office: "Tell Lewis (my oldest son) to secure all the important papers in my desk."

Early the following morning Douglass reached his home on its peaceful hill. Little ten-year-old Annie ran into his arms.

"Papa, Papa," she shouted, and burst into tears. "Oh, Papa, I'm so frightened." She clung to him desperately.

Douglass held her, saying nothing, but making deep, soothing sounds. Her thinness and uncontrollable sobbing chilled his heart.

Anna embraced him and whispered into his ear, "The child is sure that bad men will take you away, that she will never see you again. Try to calm her."

Douglass drew his daughter with him to the parlor sofa. During the past dark years of trouble Annie had been the bright streak running through his life. Now her defenselessness symbolized the smashing of his hopes.

Every method he had tried to open a crack in the monolithic power of the slave system had seemed to fail—lectures, newspapers, conventions of his people, politics, and the Underground Railroad.

The doorbell cut through his gloomy reveries. Rosetta showed in Samuel D. Porter and his neighbor, Lieutenant Governor Selden. He motioned Rosetta to take Annie out of the room. The little girl went with tears streaming silently from her eyes.

"It's not safe for you here, Frederick," said Porter, without greeting.

"I have definite information that Governor Morgan will honor the requisition from the Governor of Virginia to surrender you to the courts of that state," added Selden.

"We also know that the people of Rochester will resist any attempt by federal officers to take you away," Porter continued.

"This could lead to riots and bloodshed, which we hope to avoid," said Selden.

As each shaft struck home, Douglass remained silent. The law could no longer protect him. He must not allow the burden to fall on his friends.

He nodded in passive acceptance as Porter urged him, in the name of their long friendship, to take the familiar underground route to Canada. From there he could board the boat to England as he had planned to do, anyway, before Brown's raid.

Douglass looked out the window. The sun kept disappearing behind gray autumn clouds, draining the landscape of color. "I've always been hopeful," he said. "Now I'm not. But it lightens my heart a little to know that you and your family will be here to comfort Anna and the children."

Porter tried to smile. "I know you'll return, and sooner than you think. Surely a just God must weary of slavery. Even now its downfall may be closer than we dream."

Before the end of the day Douglass was on a boat heading across Lake Ontario to Canada. He was not alone in his flight. In nearby Peterboro Gerrit Smith had a nervous breakdown and entered a sanatorium.

Howe and Stearns also crossed the border to Canada, while Sanborn stopped off in Maine. Overseas in Italy, Parker nursed the tuberculosis from which he never recovered. Only Higginson bravely remained in Boston and would deny nothing. Of them all, Douglass had the most to fear. The sarcastic *Herald* expressed it well:

The black Douglass, having some experiences in his early life of the pleasures of Southern society, had no desire to trust himself again even on the borders of the Potomac.

Before he sailed Douglass wrote a letter to the Rochester *Democrat and American.* In it he denied the charge of one of the Harper's Ferry prisoners, John Cook, that Douglass had promised to bring a large number of men to Brown's aid. Douglass stated that he had no sympathy for slaveholders, but Brown's way of fighting slavery was not his way. " 'The tools to those who can use them!' Let every man work for the abolition of slavery in his own way."

Douglass had no apologies for keeping out of the way of the United States marshals who had come looking for him in Rochester shortly after he left the city.

A government recognizing the validity of the *Dred Scott* decision, at such a time as this, is not likely to have any very charitable feelings towards me; and if I am to meet its representatives, I prefer to do so, at least, upon equal terms.

Douglass set sail for England on November 12, 1859, aboard the liner *Scotia.* The ship had a difficult fourteen-day passage over the stormy North Atlantic. The extreme cold and the angry waves matched the grimness of Douglass's thoughts.

No one who has not himself been compelled to leave his home and country and go into permanent banishment can well imagine the state of mind and heart which such a condition brings.

Douglass did not spread this gloom to his "Readers and Friends," however, when he wrote them a farewell in his own paper. Perhaps, beyond his personal sorrow and the seeming failure of the cause he had served so long, he had some glimpse of a future promise.

From his Harper's Ferry cell, John Brown was impressing friend and foe by his courage, his dignity, his radiant love for his black brothers, and his faith in God, expressed in marvelous letters to family and friends. Perhaps Douglass already sensed something of the change by which Brown, the mad conspirator, would become Brown, the martyr of Emancipation.

> Capt. Brown has initiated a new mode of carrying on the crusade of freedom, and his blow has sent dread and terror throughout the entire ranks of the piratical army of slavery. His daring deeds may cost him his life, but priceless as is the value of that life, the blow he has struck, will, in the end, prove to be worth its mighty cost. Like Samson, he has laid his hands upon the pillars of this great national temple of cruelty and blood, and when he falls, that temple will speedily crumble to its final doom, burying its denizens in its ruins.

13 a fateful election

*The slaveholders themselves have saved our cause from ruin! They
have exposed the throat of slavery to the keen knife of liberty . . . .*
Frederick Douglass

The election of 1860 was drawing to a climax. Frederick Douglass, who had been back in Rochester since May, shared the
intense interest of his fellow Americans in their most exciting
presidential campaign in twenty years.

Douglass had interrupted his tour of the British Isles
when he received word of a personal tragedy, the first ever to
darken his Rochester home. His little Annie, learning of the
death of the kind old man on whose knee she had so often sat,
and pining for the father she feared never to see again, had
fallen ill. She lost the power to speak or hear. Her whole family
was convinced she died of a broken heart.

Douglass's good friends in England, like the Richardsons
and Julia Griffiths Crofts, had tried to persuade him to stay.
His lectures were reviving the anti-slavery spirit in Great Britain. His life would be in danger if he returned. But Douglass
was determined to rejoin his family in their mutual grief. He
slipped quietly back into Rochester by way of Canada.

Douglass soon found that such caution had become un-
necessary. No one wished to arrest him any longer for his connection with John Brown. As Douglass had prophesied in
November, the martyrdom of this one man had converted
more people to anti-slavery than the thirty years of agitation by
the abolitionists.

Not only had the Republicans nominated an anti-slavery

Abraham Lincoln in 1860

man, Abraham Lincoln, under their banner of "No More Slave States," but he actually had a good chance to win. His opponents were divided three ways. There were proslavery Southern Democrats and Northern Democrats indifferent to slavery, led by Lincoln's old rival, Senator Stephen A. Douglas of Illinois. There was even a Constitutional Union party which stood vaguely for "the Union and the Constitution."

Lincoln was not an abolitionist. However, Douglass pointed out with pleasure, he was:

> a man of unblemished private character . . . has a cool, well balanced head; great firmness of will; is perseveringly industrious; and one of the most frank, honest men in political life.

Why then did Douglass fail to come out wholeheartedly in support of Lincoln and the Republicans? Lincoln himself,

like his party, like most Northerners, suffered from a fatally
ambiguous attitude toward the Negro.

Lincoln had been born in the South and had grown up
in Indiana. He was morally opposed to slavery. Yet he was
swayed by the slavery-inspired notion of the natural inferiority
of the Negro. The black man should be free to eat the bread
he had earned with his own hands, but he could never be the
civil and social equal of the white man.

The Republican party of New York State showed its true
colors when it refused to support a complete Negro suffrage
amendment which was appearing on the ballot for the first
time in thirteen years. Douglass and his New York City friends,
like James McCune Smith, threw most of their campaigning
energy into supporting this amendment. If passed, it would
abolish the requirement that a black man must own $250
worth of property to vote.

As election day drew near, Douglass sensed more and more
that the future of his people was bound up with the election
of Lincoln. Lincoln did not campaign in his own behalf. Such
conduct was considered undignified for a presidential candidate. He stayed home in Springfield, Illinois, issuing policy
statements from time to time.

Lincoln's banner was carried by young volunteers called
"Wide-Awake." Often Douglass saw them on autumn evenings, leading torchlight parades, chanting rousing songs, and
holding mass rallies. They flung back the taunts of the Democratic "Little Giants" about the "Railsplitter." They stressed
that simple-hearted "Honest Abe," the log-cabin candidate,
understood the problems of the workingman and the new
immigrants.

On November 6, 1860, Douglass stood all day in front of
the polls in Rochester. He passed out a pamphlet prepared by
James McCune Smith and the New York City and County
Suffrage Committee for Colored Citizens. It asked white New
Yorkers the question:

Is it not a shame for our state, that in 1777, when it was perilous to life to be a citizen of New York, she made colored men citizens, and that afterwards, in 1821, when it was safe and honorable to be a citizen, she disfranchised her colored citizens? Let us entreat you, remove this reproach from the fair fame of our noble state.

Many well-known citizens who came to cast ballots stopped to shake hands with Douglass. But there were dissenters.

Presently a local ward heeler herded in a group of workmen, fresh from the tavern, some barely able to speak English. Douglass heard the ward heeler warning them that the "niggers" were out to get their jobs. They pushed Douglass's pamphlet roughly aside.

Great was Douglass's astonishment to see one of the most unshaven workmen slip back toward him, waving a ballot. Without a word of apology he asked Douglass to read the ballot for him. Douglass complied wearily. No one had suggested that this white workman be deprived of his vote because of his poverty and ignorance.

It reminded Douglass of Gardiner's shipyard. As long as politicians encouraged hostility between white and black workers, whose interests were really the same, the black workers would be trapped in their poverty while the white workers bettered their condition.

The results of the voting left Douglass torn between joy and discouragement. Lincoln had won by a heavy electoral margin and with a substantial lead over his nearest opponent. Yet even the Republicans who had voted for Lincoln had not seen fit to support the Negro suffrage amendment. It had been rejected 337, 984 to 197, 503.

"The black baby of Negro Suffrage was thought too ugly to exhibit on so grand an occasion," Douglass wrote in his December *Monthly*. But, he warned the Republicans, "you are not done with us yet."

As Douglass analyzed the election for his readers, he expressed gratitude that Northerners had finally found the courage to vote their anti-slavery principles. He noted the fearful frenzy of the South and the threats of disunion, and all because of Lincoln's proposal to stop only the *extension* of slavery: " 'Minutemen' are forming, drums are beating, flags are flying, people are arming, 'banks are closing,' 'stocks are falling' ". . . .

The hysteria of the South spread to the Northern merchants—the price of cotton would fall, the mills would close. And it was all because of the abolitionists, they told their ward heelers and dock foremen. Because of these abolitionists you'll lose your jobs. War will come and you'll lose your lives as well.

Douglass arrived in Boston on December 3 to address a meeting in Tremont Temple, commemorating the death of John Brown. For over twenty-five years, since Garrison had been harassed by a mob, free speech had gone unmolested in Boston. But today as he approached the temple Douglass was aware of baleful looks from the crowd. There were cries of "Hang the abolitionists! They're causing all the trouble!"

Douglass hurried inside and down the aisle to the platform. Then he stopped short. Next to the only vacant chair among the speakers was a familiar figure, as elegant as ever. It was Wendell Phillips. His sandy hair had retreated farther from his high forehead and become streaked with gray, but his blue eyes held the same unwavering light.

While Douglass hesitated, Phillips walked straight over to his old friend. He wrung Douglass's hand with that well-remembered kindliness that conveyed warmth without any trace of intimacy.

"There are some who grow timid, confused, in the hour of danger," said Phillips. "I know your courage is equal to the times."

Douglass, overcome with surprise and emotion, could only smile his agreement.

During the burst of applause that greeted Douglass's first

attempt to speak, there came a louder roar from the back of the hall. A mob surged in and down the aisles. Chairs were thrown and ladies screamed.

Six or eight men converged on Douglass and began to pummel him with their fists. Roused to fury, Douglass hammered back blow for blow like a "trained pugilist." But he was hopelessly outnumbered and was thrown from the platform to the floor of the hall. Fortunately he was only stunned. Phillips hurried over to help him to his feet.

The audience rushed out like a defeated army. A larger mob was waiting in front of the ornate Gothic temple. They singled out the Negroes for attack and several were badly beaten. But Douglass and Phillips, refusing to be silenced, led the audience to the Joy Street Baptist Church, where the meeting began again.

When his turn came to speak, Douglass had quite recovered. He referred jokingly to Phillips's belated support for *all* methods of fighting slavery—"politics, religion, peace, war, Bible, Constitution, Disunion, Union. . . ." Douglass, from his own bitter experience, was becoming convinced that there was only one way left—all others had been tried and failed. It was time "to reach the slaveholder's conscience through his fear of personal danger."

Finally, he referred to his happy reunion with Phillips in yielding the floor to

> a friend on my right, whose voice to-night I have not heard for many years past. These troublous times in which we live, and have been living for a few years past, make that voice doubly dear to me on this occasion. . . .

To Douglass, thinking over the events of the night, the most depressing aspect of the mob was not the ignorant rowdies, who were only following their normal trade; it was the gentlemen in broadcloth suits and high silk hats whom he had glimpsed directing the attacks.

Abolitionists, commemorating the death of John Brown, are driven from Tremont Temple by a mob. (From Harper's Weekly)

On December 10, at the Music Hall, Douglass commented on the mob and its work and made one of his finest appeals for free speech:·

> Until the right is accorded to the humblest as freely as to the most exalted citizen, the government of Boston is but an empty name, and its freedom a mockery. A man's right to speak does not depend upon where he was born or upon his color. The simple quality of manhood is the solid basis of the right—and there let it rest forever.

Douglass and Phillips had need of all their courage and determination in the next three trying months. Both were the objects of abuse. Phillips was followed for three days by a howling mob everywhere he went on the streets of Boston.

In those days a new president did not take office until March 4. Beginning in late December with South Carolina, the states of the Deep South began to secede from the Union. President Buchanan's reaction was the same as it had been to every crisis of his administration—give in to the South, do absolutely nothing.

Panic and doubt gripped the North. Peace conferences were called in which even anti-slavery men were willing to make slavery perpetual if the South would not secede.

Instead the South proceeded to elect Jefferson Davis President of the Confederate States of America. The rebels took over every fort and stockpile of the United States government in the South except Fort Sumter in Charleston Harbor.

By the time Lincoln was traveling East for the inauguration, conspiracy and threat had drawn a net of danger around him. On the advice of Allan Pinkerton, the detective, Lincoln had to travel to the Capital at night and in disguise. In such a climate Lincoln's inaugural address was bound to disappoint abolitionists like Douglass. The new president barely mentioned slavery. His strongest words were that the Union was perpetual and could not be broken up.

Just at this moment of despair, Douglass received an invitation to visit Haiti. Though he had never approved of American Negroes emigrating to other lands, his spirits revived at the thought of visiting the first black republic. He agreed to sail from New York on April 21.

The news of Fort Sumter caught Douglass packing for Haiti and writing his editorials for the May issue of his *Monthly*. He hurried downstairs to tell his family that he no longer intended to go to Haiti. He had work to do at home. Lewis, his oldest son, spoke up. He intended to enlist.

Douglass shook his head sadly; it was too early for the government to take such a radical step. Once again he must act as a goad to the conscience of the nation and the president. He returned to his desk to write a new editorial. In it he sounded the call that he was to repeat tirelessly for the first two years of the war:

> *Let the slaves and free colored people be called into service, and formed into a liberating army*, to march into the South and raise the banner of Emancipation among the slaves.

14 **day of jubilee**

*The day dawns—the morning star is bright upon the horizon! The
iron gate of our prison stands half open. One gallant rush from the
North will fling it wide open, while four millions of our brothers and
sisters shall march out into liberty.*

Frederick Douglass

On July 4, 1862, Frederick Douglass rose with a heavy heart
to address a crowd of two thousand gathered on the town
square in Himrods Corners, New York. Over a year after Fort
Sumter, it did not seem to Douglass that he had made much
progress in his two-pronged attack on the government's faint-
hearted war policy. The slaves had not been freed, except in
the District of Columbia. No Negro volunteers had been permitted to enlist in the army.

Many craned their necks to see the famous orator who,
despite the hot sun, looked cool and self-possessed in his white
summer linen. The gray that shot through his mane of black
hair emphasized the undercurrent of sadness in his manner.
He told the crowd that he could no longer bite his tongue to
keep from criticizing Lincoln. The government was throwing
away its chance at victory by failing to attack the root cause of
the war.

> This slavery begotten and slavery sustained, and
> slavery animated war, has now cost this nation more than
> a hundred thousand lives and more than five hundred
> millions of treasure. It has weighed down the national
> heart with sorrow and heaviness, such as no speech can
> portray. It has cast doubt upon the possibility of liberty
> and self-government which it will require a century to
> remove.—The question is, shall this stupendous and most
> outrageous war be finally and forever ended? Or shall it be

merely suspended for a time, and again revived with increased and aggravated fury in the future?

Unknown to Douglass, Lincoln was coming to the same conclusion. Slavery must go. But before the North would accept such a move he must stem the tide of defeat that had dogged Northern armies since the start of the war.

General McClellan's inconclusive victory at Antietam gave Lincoln the excuse he needed. On September 22 he called his cabinet together to read them the preliminary draft of the most earthshaking document since the Constitution—the Emancipation Proclamation.

On the morning of September 23 Douglass read with widening eyes and unbelieving joy the words of President Lincoln:

> That on the first day of January, . . . [1863], all persons held as slaves within any State or designated part of a State the people whereof shall then be in rebellion against the United States, shall be then, thenceforward, and forever free. . . .

"Forever free." Was it possible? Douglass looked out the window at the golden September sun, warm upon the still-green leaves and the late-blooming gardens of suburban homes. From a full heart Douglass poured out his joy on paper at this dizzy turn of events:

> "Free forever." oh! long enslaved millions, whose cries have so vexed the air and sky, suffer on a few more days in sorrow, the hour of your deliverance draws nigh! Oh! Ye millions of free and loyal men who have earnestly sought to free your bleeding country from the dreadful ravages of revolution and anarchy, lift up now your voices with joy and thanksgiving for with freedom to the slave will come peace and safety to your country.

Anna E. Dickinson

On the evening of January 1, 1863, Douglass came out of his boardinghouse in Boston to find a new-fallen snow frosting the earth. As so often in the past, he was making his way across Boston Common to Tremont Temple. The meeting he was attending, the last of three sponsored by the Union Progressive Associations, had been called to wait for, and, possibly to celebrate, the issuance of the great proclamation.

The painful suspense of the last three months had been continued through the day's earlier meetings. It was not expected that Lincoln would sign the document till after he had shaken hundreds of hands at the New Year's afternoon reception in the White House. There were still many who feared he would not sign it at all.

Suppose his wife's Southern birth should sway him? Suppose he should be deterred by the continuing opposition of so many Northerners? Suppose his well-known fondness for compromise should cause him to give the South one more chance?

Douglass forgot all these supposings as he moved along, his way lit by the unearthly glow of the oil lamps gilding the new-fallen snow. Full of hope, he hurried down the aisles of the temple. His old friend William Wells Brown wrung his hand. J. Sella Martin, an eloquent Negro preacher, stood by to welcome him. New to the abolition ranks was a beautiful young white girl of nineteen—Anna E. Dickinson, who had been fired from her job at the United States mint in 1861 because of her anti-slavery views.

At eight o'clock the first speaker rose. Douglass, Brown, Anna Dickinson, and Martin each talked in turn. But each sensed he was only marking time. Every ear was straining for a different message. Black and white, all were waiting for the sound of feet pounding over the pavement with the long-promised words. A string of messengers had been posted at short intervals between the telegraph office and the temple.

Nine o'clock came and went; the audience began to grow restless. Overhead the great chandeliers radiated into the points of a star, casting a jewellike light on the intricate Gothic carvings of the temple. But the audience was blind to their beauty.

It was nearly ten o'clock. Douglass whispered to Brown, "We must do something. They are losing heart."

As if in answer to his plea, there was a rush over the cobblestones. A messenger streaked down the aisle to the platform. "It is coming! It is coming!" he cried. "It's on the wires."

There was a shout of joy that threatened to lift the roof of the temple. When the next messenger brought the complete text, it could hardly be heard above the cheering. The slaves were to be freed and, at long last, Negro volunteers to be called:

And upon this act, sincerely believed to be an act of justice, warranted by the Constitution upon military necessity, I invoke the considerate judgment of mankind and the gracious favor of Almighty God.

When the last words rang out, it was as if the lungs of every man and woman in the audience had been freed from the same bonds that had chained the slave. Some laughed; some wept; some shouted for joy; some sat silent and stunned as if the happiness were too deep for any utterance. Expressing the emotion of those thousands, Douglass burst into the anthem, "Blow the Trumpet, Blow." Everyone joined in like a mighty human organ swelling with one united voice.

Rue, an old Negro preacher who had waited silently all those hours, took up the chorus. With a strong, if unsteady, voice, he led the jubilant singers in:

Sound the loud timbrel o'er Egypt's dark sea,
Jehovah has triumphed, his people are free.

At midnight, when the temple was scheduled to close, the excitement and the volume of singing were still rising. The Reverend Leonard Grimes, a Negro minister who had been imprisoned in Virginia for helping fugitives, offered the use of his Twelfth Baptist Church on Phillips Street.

All the most fervent celebrants crowded into the church within an hour, Douglass included. The jubilee went on till early in the morning. When Douglass came out of the church, dawn was already beginning to turn the black sky to gray. But he was experiencing one of those exalted moods when a man feels no weariness.

The black communities in other cities throughout the North were as eager as the Bostonians to celebrate the great deliverance. Douglass was in constant demand as a speaker.

The Reverend Henry Highland Garnet

In the month of January he traveled two thousand miles in a jagged path from Boston to Chicago, speaking "almost without interruption."

Douglass returned to Rochester in early February, hoarse and weary. For the first time he examined the proclamation in the cold light of day. Not a single slave gained immediate freedom from it. The slaves in the border states, then under Union control, were not emancipated at all. Yet Douglass felt that it contained "in its spirit a life and power beyond its letter."

His optimism increased when he received an important visitor on February 23. It was George L. Stearns, the wealthy Boston abolitionist who had supported John Brown. Stearns, now a major, had been appointed chief recruiting officer for the Fifty-fourth Massachusetts Infantry Regiment by Governor John A. Andrew of Massachusetts. It was to be the first Negro regiment recruited among the free blacks of the North. A regiment of ex-slaves had already been formed in South Carolina under Douglass's friend, Col. Thomas Wentworth Higginson.

Stearns hoped that Douglass would join other black leaders like Henry Highland Garnet, J. W. Loguen, William Wells Brown, and Charles Lenox Remond in raising the quota of young volunteers as quickly as possible.

At last Douglass had the assignment he had been waiting to fill for two long, dreary years. When he told Lewis and Charles of his new work, both volunteered to be among the first young men from New York to join the regiment.

Douglass warned them, "You will be severely criticized and even insulted. You will be fighting a double battle—against slavery at the South and against prejudice at the North. But do not lose heart. I think our success is sure."

Douglass prepared to leave Rochester on his recruiting tour. But first he issued a famous enlistment call that was reprinted all over the North:

MEN OF COLOR, TO ARMS!

When first the Rebel cannon shattered the walls of Sumter, and drove away its starving garrison, I predicted that the war then and there inaugurated would not be fought out entirely by white men. Every month's experience during these two dreary years has confirmed that opinion. A war undertaken and brazenly carried on for the perpetual enslavement of colored men, calls logically and loudly upon colored men to help suppress it. . . . Slowly and reluctantly that appeal is beginning to be heeded. Stop not now to complain that it was not heeded sooner. . . . Action! action! not criticism, is the plain duty of this hour. Words are now useful only as they stimulate to blows. The office of speech now is only to point out when, where and how to strike to the best advantage. There is no time for delay. The tide is at flood that leads on to fortune. . . . Liberty won by white men would lack half its lustre. . . . The counsel I give comes of close observation of the great struggle now in progress—and of the deep conviction that this is your hour and mine.

In good earnest, then, and after the best deliberation, I, now, for the first time during the war, feel at liberty to call and counsel you to arms. By every consideration which binds you to your enslaved fellow countrymen, and the peace and welfare of your country; by every aspiration which you cherish for the freedom and equality of yourselves and your children; by all the ties of blood and identity which make us one with the brave black men now fighting our battles in Louisiana, in South Carolina, I urge you to fly to arms, and smite with death the power that would bury the Government and your liberty in the same hopeless grave.

On a day late in May the sun shone brilliantly on the green grass of Boston Common. The stars and stripes were flying from every building and pole in the city. One hundred policemen lined the streets to hold back the crowds in anticipation of trouble. Yet the mood of the people was expectant and excited, not fearful.

By the time the distant music of drums and bugles was heard from the downtown streets, the crowds numbered twenty thousand. The color guard of the Fifty-fourth Massachusetts Infantry Regiment came into view. The American flag, the flag of the state, and the regimental colors were carried proudly by the three black soldiers at the head. Instead of the jeers and catcalls that had recently greeted them here, there were only cheers and applause. The precision of the marching men in their blue Union uniforms won the immediate admiration of the crowds.

As the spirited troops passed Wendell Phillips's house on Essex Street, they saw William Lloyd Garrison. He stood on the balcony at Phillips's side, his hand resting upon a bust of John Brown.

Among the most excited spectators was Frederick Douglass. He followed the line of march from the train station to the Common, trying to keep the brave sight of Lewis and

Charles in their uniforms always in view. Lewis, as sergeant major, had the highest rank of any black soldier. Whatever difficulties they might have to endure, at least the colored troops were now badly needed. General enlistments had dropped sharply among white men.

The regiment drew up on the Common before the ever-growing crowd. The young, ardent white colonel, Robert Gould Shaw, just graduated from Harvard, looked slim and boyish as he presented his men to Governor John A. Andrew.

With the review over, Douglass followed the men down to the Battery Wharf to the tune of "John Brown's Body." Shaw and the other officers, fearing hostile demonstrations en route, had decided that the regiment should travel to South Carolina by sea. A new ship, the *De Molay*, waited at anchor, and Douglass boarded her with his sons and their comrades-in-arms.

Douglass remained on deck while the sailors cast her off from her moorings and she moved well out into the crowded harbor. When the tug which had guided the *De Molay* toward the open ocean was preparing to return home, Douglass had to go, too. He bid Godspeed to Colonel Shaw. He gave a last quick embrace to Charles and Lewis. He promised to bear their greetings to their mother and sister and Lewis's fiancée Amelia Loguen, daughter of his friend Bishop J. W. Loguen of Syracuse.

Douglass climbed the ladder to the tug. The water quickly separated the two ships as the tug steamed back to port. Douglass watched as long as he could. The last thing he saw was the glint of the sun on the golden eagle of Colonel Shaw's hat.

15 rights of black soldiers

We are fighting for something incomparably better than the old Union. We are fighting for unity; unity of idea, unity of sentiment, unity of object, unity of institutions, in which there shall be no North, no South, no East, no West, no black, no white, but a solidarity of the nation, making every slave free, and every free man a voter.

Frederick Douglass

Frederick Douglass was back in the newspaper office in Rochester on a stifling July day. In his hand was a copy of his latest recruiting speech, given in Philadelphia. He planned to include it in his August *Monthly*. For the first time he had had trouble enlisting young men from the black community.

Just then the door of the office swung open without a knock. Amelia Loguen, Lewis's fiancée, who had been visiting in Rochester, flung it back and rushed in, waving a newspaper. Her eyes were red-rimmed and swollen.

Douglass took the paper from her and read it with a sinking heart. He knew that the Massachusetts Fifty-fourth had been fighting before Charleston ever since arriving from Boston. On July 18, according to the report, they had been ordered to attack Fort Wagner, one of the strongest links in the harbor defenses.

The men of the Fifty-fourth were sick and exhausted from constant fighting and forced marches. Despite their weakened condition, they had swept over the parapets and stormed the fort. They were raked by a murderous fire from the defenders. Even so, the Fifty-fourth fought with such tenacity that they might have carried the day, but no reserves were standing by to back them up. Colonel Shaw was killed along with hundreds of his men, and buried with them in a common grave. Many others were taken prisoner and reportedly sold into slavery.

Douglass dropped the paper and took Amelia's small, cool hand in his big, warm ones. He closed his eyes against the dread vision of Lewis and Charles dead, dying, or being dragged to the auction block.

Suddenly Douglass smote the desk top with his fist. He told Amelia that not one more poor, brave, trusting black man should he recruit until he had brought their wrongs and sufferings before the highest authority in the land. He sat down to write Major Stearns that he could not attend the recruiting rally in Pittsburgh. He could no longer recruit with a clear conscience. The government must take steps to improve the treatment of Negro troops at once.

The next week was a grim one at the house on South Avenue. Then two important letters arrived on the same day. The first, from Lewis, informed his parents that he was safe (Charles was unharmed as well).

> The splendid 54th is cut to pieces. . . . I had my sword sheath blown away while on the parapet of the Fort. The grape and canister . . . shell and minnies swept us down like chaff, still our men went on, . . . and if we had been properly supported, we would have held the Fort, but the white troops could not be made to come up. The consequence was we had to fall back. . . .

An even more astonishing letter came for Douglass from Major Stearns. He had reason to believe that Lincoln and Secretary of War Stanton were so deeply concerned about the raising of Negro troops that they might be willing to grant Douglass an interview.

Douglass was still incredulous as he drove to the White House on a late July day in a carriage with Senator Pomeroy of Kansas. For the first time in many years Douglass was acutely aware of the degradation from which he had risen. He found the steps to the president's office crowded as usual with petitioners and job seekers. Before the days of civil service exams, the president had to waste many hours giving out patronage to his party.

Douglass and Pomeroy squeezed past the crowds to the door of the president's office, where Douglass handed his card to Col. John Hay, one of Lincoln's secretaries. Sour looks followed his every move. Douglass supposed he would have to wait half the day. To his surprise his name was called within two minutes. Behind him he heard one of the disappointed hangers-on mutter, "You might know *he* would get in before us."

The massive door swung slowly open. The tall, lanky president was "sitting in his usual position . . . with his feet in different parts of the room," as Douglass later described the scene. Lincoln rose at once and waved aside Pomeroy's introductions.

"Mr. Douglass, I know you," he said. "I have read about you and Mr. Seward has told me about you."

The president's sincerity and lack of formality put Douglass instantly at ease. "Sit down; I am glad to see you," he continued, pointing to a chair.

Douglass sat down, feeling far more at home than he expected. Yet he was a little awed by a sense of the nearness of great decisions of state and the terrible burdens of office. Everywhere were reminders of the work that went on relentlessly, day and night. Piles of paper stood on desks and chairs. Two young secretaries were busy taking notes, looking weary. The deep lines of worry and sadness on Lincoln's forehead were by now ineradicably engraved there.

Yet Lincoln spoke with perfect good humor of a speech Douglass had recently made, accusing the administration of a "hesitating, vacillating policy." He admitted he might sometimes be slow, "but I think it can not be shown that when I have once taken a position, I have ever retreated from it."

Douglass came straight to the point. "As I'm sure you're aware, Mr. President, I have been for several months past assisting to raise colored troops. Many, including my own sons, have been glad to answer your call. But now I find it almost impossible to sign up a single man. They feel that the government has not been dealing fairly with them in several important matters."

"I should like to hear their reasons." Lincoln sat back quietly with his hands folded, his face grave and attentive, his manner sympathetic. In the midst of the hectic activity swirling about him, he acted as if he had all the time in the world.

Douglass stated that in the first place black troops should receive the same pay as white ones. Secondly, the Rebels should be forced to treat captured black soldiers as prisoners of war. If necessary, the United States should retaliate against captured Rebel soldiers if Negro soldiers continued to be killed and enslaved. Finally, Negro soldiers who distinguished themselves in battle should receive the same honors and promotions as white soldiers.

Douglass saw that Lincoln was sincerely troubled by his words. "Mr. Douglass," he said, "I understand very well how you feel and how the colored soldiers feel. Yet our using them at all is a great advance; many still criticize me for enlisting them. After all, they have much greater reason for fighting than white men and ought to be willing to do so under any conditions. Yet, I assure you that in the end they shall have the same pay as white soldiers."

Douglass's second point seemed to give Lincoln the greatest difficulty. He was distressed that captured Negro troops were not treated as prisoners of war; he was equally distressed at the thought of retaliating against innocent men because of their treatment. "Once begun I do not know where such a measure would stop."

The last point was the easiest for Lincoln to approve. Though he made no definite promise, he said he would be glad to sign any commissions for black officers that came across his desk.

When Douglass shook hands with Lincoln and left the room, he realized the president had given him new hope. He had received no solid promises to support such a hope. Yet Lincoln's honesty and integrity seemed to him now beyond question. Moreover, he had never once been reminded of his humble origins or unpopular color, but had been received "as one gentleman receives another," he later told his friends.

Douglass's next stop was the War Department. No contrast could have been greater than that between the kind and courteous Lincoln and the prickly, impatient Stanton. The secretary bustled about the room, talking in short, sharp sentences to several officials already seated there. He was a heavily bearded man, shorter than Lincoln and rather portly, who peered at his guest from under gloomy brows. That look seemed to say, Well, what is it? Come to the point at once.

Fortunately, Stanton was as efficient and hardworking and devoted as he was ill-mannered. Douglass described briefly his meeting with Lincoln. Quite suddenly, Stanton's suspicious and harried expression changed. He focused all his attention on Douglass.

"Your recruiting must go on, Mr. Douglass. It is vital." Stanton's arm chopped at the air to emphasize his words. "The best way for the colored man to win his freedom and his citizenship is by fighting for it on the battlefield. Equal pay, better treatment will soon follow."

"The president has offered to sign any commissions that come across his desk. I would be willing to accept one." Douglass had always lived by the principle: "Power concedes nothing without a demand."

Stanton knitted his brows. "I could make you assistant adjutant on the staff of Gen. Lorenzo Thomas, adjutant general. He is assigned to raise new recruits in the Mississippi Valley."

Douglass thanked Stanton for his consideration and left. He could hardly wait to tell Anna the good news of his commission. And, of course, the last issue of *Douglass' Monthly* must be completed.

A couple of days later Douglass sat at his familiar desk in the corner of the newspaper office. Sadness colored his letter of farewell to his readers, though he welcomed the new challenge. For sixteen years all his best hopes had been tied up in the struggle to keep the paper alive.

Douglass thought of his words flying across the country and the sea for the last time to readers who had become friends. His work, he explained to them, was not done. Rather, the fate of slavery was now in the hands of the god of battles. Moreover, now that anti-slavery was respectable, several papers like New York's *Tribune* and *Independent* would publish any article he might write. As a last goodbye he wrote:

> With a heart full and warm with gratitude to you for all you have done in furtherance of the cause of these to whom I have devoted my life, I bid you an affectionate farewell.

Douglass had burned his bridges in vain. On August 13 he received a letter from the War Department. He was to report to General Thomas, but not one word was said about his exact duties or position. No commission for Douglass ever came. And he was too aware of the importance of rank in the army to go to war without some mark of it on his shoulders.

Someone in the administration had evidently considered the move too radical. By the end of the war there were a few Negro officers in uniform, including the adventurous Martin R. Delany. But for Douglass, the lecture platform again became a battle outpost.

After all, Douglass realized, his speaking might yet accomplish more for the black man than any service he could perform in an army camp. The slaves had not really been freed by the Emancipation Proclamation.

As the Union armies approached their plantations, thousands of slaves vanished from the fields and kitchens and parlors. They believed "Massa Linkum" had made them free. But actually nothing was sure about their postwar status.

Douglass, like Phillips, wanted to be certain that Negro soldiers came marching home to true citizenship, and not to slavery under another name. Above all, the black man must win the right to vote.

Since his interview with Lincoln, however, Douglass had greater faith in him as a man. In the president's seeming humility and simplicity, Douglass had sensed his future greatness. He believed that Lincoln was close to the heart of the people. When Lincoln became convinced that the people would accept more rights for Negroes, Lincoln would grant them, regardless of opposition. So Douglass, in his now highly popular lectures, sought to win more Northerners to his twin objectives —freedom for the slaves and equal rights for all black men.

In 1864 Americans were faced with a presidential election in the midst of a desperate and bloody war. Lincoln was renominated by acclamation, but there was much underground opposition.

The war seemed to have reached a stalemate. Just when it was evident that the South could not possibly win, many in the North believed she could not be beaten. Sherman was stalled at the gates of Atlanta. Grant was held at bay in the Wilderness of northern Virginia.

In this defeatist mood, many Republicans felt that Lincoln had no chance of winning. The mood of national gloom naturally affected Douglass.

On a warm day in early August visitors knocked at the door of the house on South Avenue. Elizabeth Chace, her eighteen-year-old daughter, Lillie, and Amy and Isaac Post were ushered into the parlor by Rosetta, now Mrs. Nathan Sprague. The Chaces had stopped by on their way from Niagara Falls.

Anna Murray Douglass

Lillie was excited at the thought of seeing a man who was almost a legend in her household. Douglass and Mrs. Chace had not met in the long years since his quarrel with the Garrisonians. But Douglass's books were on her shelf and an early portrait hung on the wall in the Chace home.

Lillie caught her breath at the magnificent figure that stood before her. Douglass seemed to her to surpass humanity. Mrs. Chace's greeting was full of womanly dignity and gentleness. Douglass bowed over her hand with a "magnificent movement of haughty courtesy."

"There are no friends like the old friends," said Douglass. He acknowledged the greetings of the Posts and smiled at Lillie when she curtsied. But all his words were really for Mrs. Chace alone.

"Frederick, can I not see thy wife? I have never met her."

Douglass pointed to the beautiful garden where Anna was sitting in the sun. Arthritic attacks were beginning to disable her. Douglass presented her to Mrs. Chace and Lillie with courtly grace.

Then the two old friends strolled through the garden paths, admiring the view down to the Genesee. Suddenly Lillie's ears pricked up. Her mother's voice came to her, soft but very clear. "Frederick, why have I seen nothing of thee in all these years?"

The answer came in a voice like distant thunder. "Because you sided with Garrison."

"Yes, I thought Garrison was right, but it didn't make any difference to my feeling for thee. I loved thee, Frederick, just the same."

Douglass saw Mrs. Chace many times thereafter, and they remained friends to the end of their lives.

Before this visit ended Douglass told Mrs. Chace how disturbed he was by the continuing inequalities in the treatment of black soldiers. True, they were now paid the same as white soldiers, but they still suffered from inferior arms and training, excessive fatigue duty, and menial labor.

But, most of all, Douglass was outraged by the treatment of captured Negro soldiers by the Confederates. A rebel army under Gen. Nathan B. Forrest, a former slave trader, had tortured and slaughtered the black defenders of Fort Pillow even after they had surrendered.

Douglass wished he might see Lincoln again. He had been favorably impressed by the man even though he did not always approve his policies. Douglass had recently conveyed his doubts to John Eaton. Eaton, a chaplain, was on his way to Washington to report to Lincoln about his work among the freed slaves in Tennessee.

John Eaton *did* tell Lincoln of Douglass's doubts about the government policy toward Negro soldiers. Lincoln said he would like to see Douglass again:

> considering the condition from which he had arisen and the obstacles that he had overcome, and the position to which he had attained that he regarded him one of the most meritorious men, if not the most meritorious man in the United States. . . .

August 19 was a sultry midsummer day. By afternoon black clouds had obscured the blazing sun, softening the ragged outlines of wartime Washington—the unfinished buildings, the soldiers encamped on the green, the dusty streets.

Frederick Douglass sat down in a corner of the White House reception room and picked up a book. It was as dark as evening. Another visitor, Joseph T. Mills, became so fascinated by the remarkable profile of the man reading that he stood stock still and stared. Douglass felt the intensity of Mills's look. He glanced into the eyes of his observer.

Mills stammered, "Are you the president?"

"No, I am Frederick Douglass."

Just then Colonel Hay called Douglass's name. The president greeted him like an old friend. Douglass felt his admiration for the president flooding back and deepening. In Lincoln's

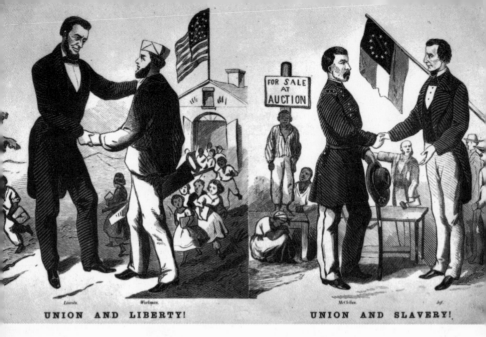

UNION AND LIBERTY!   UNION AND SLAVERY!

1864 political cartoon—Lincoln represents "Union and Liberty" while McClellan, with Jefferson Davis, stands for "Union and Slavery."

intensely human face, he saw reflected the country's sufferings. Yet the sufferings that the war had caused did not prevent Lincoln from sticking to the course he felt was right. For the first time he told Douglass that he did not think the Union could be truly restored unless slavery were abolished.

"Yet I fear all these peace moves may force me to act against my will," said Lincoln. "If the war should end before the South is defeated, I am concerned for the fate of the slaves in the rebelling states."

Douglass was both flattered and saddened by Lincoln's frank confession. Lincoln wished Douglass to organize a sort of Underground Railroad on the border of the South, and to bring as many slaves as possible within the Union lines. Douglass promised to discuss this with other black leaders.

Just then Hay announced for a second time "Governor Buckingham of Connecticut," a loyal Union man.

Lincoln replied, "Tell the governor to wait, for I want to have a long talk with my friend Frederick Douglass."

As soon as he left the president, Douglass hurried home to Rochester. He sent Lincoln a letter giving a detailed outline for a plan in which one general agent and twenty-five men would initiate the slave-running plan.

The same day, August 29, the Democrats in Chicago nominated McClellan for president on a peace-at-any-price platform. And on September 2, Sherman entered Atlanta.

Everything was changed for the Union as well as for Douglass by these two events. If the abolitionists had hesitated to support Lincoln, they no longer did so when the alternative was McClellan and the Peace Democrats. With victory marching through Georgia on the heels of Sherman's relentless army, there was no more need for underground railroads.

On October 4 Douglass, Garnet, Langston, and all the important black leaders met at Syracuse. They endorsed Lincoln. But they also reminded the Republicans that the liberties of black men must be secured. The right to vote was the "keystone of the arch of human liberty."

In the official report, written by Douglass, there was a prophecy. He predicted that the South would cherish a "sacred animosity" against the government which would be passed on from father to son. Since the North could not win the loyalty of the masters, it should at least secure the loyalty of the slaves.

Lincoln won by a heavy electoral vote of 212 to 21. His popular margin, however, was only 400,000 out of 4,000,000 votes cast.

In the winter of 1864-65 Grant was hammering back Lee in Virginia, fighting for every acre of ground. For the first time in almost thirty years Douglass came as far south as Baltimore on his lecture tour.

At the end of his first lecture a gray-haired but erect Negro woman approached him. In a minute he was warmly grasping the hand of his sister Eliza. They hadn't met since both had worked in Master Thomas's kitchen in St. Michaels.

"Our meeting," he wrote a friend later, "can be better imagined than described."

In her own quiet way Eliza had shown the same determined spirit as her brother. She had bought herself and her nine children out of slavery. His brother, Perry, and other sisters had been sold south. She was in touch with Master Thomas, all the Hugh Aulds having died. Master Thomas had expressed interest in meeting Douglass. Douglass, however, felt such a meeting would be awkward. How could he and his former master address each other?

The emotions awakened by meeting his sister gave way to excitement of a different sort. On March 4, 1865, Douglass and Mrs. Thomas Dorsey stood among the crowds in front of the Capitol steps. Lincoln took the oath of office for a second time and delivered the immortal words:

> Fondly do we hope—fervently do we pray—that this mighty scourge of war may speedily pass away. Yet, if God wills that it continue until all the wealth piled by the bondman's two hundred and fifty years of unrequited toil shall be sunk, and until every drop of blood drawn with the lash shall be paid by another drawn with the sword, as was said three thousand years ago, so still it must be said, "The judgments of the Lord are true and righteous altogether."
>
> With malice toward none; with charity for all; with firmness in the right, as God gives us to see the right, let us strive on to finish the work we are in; to bind up the nation's wounds; to care for him who shall have borne the battle, and for his widow, and his orphan—to do all which may achieve and cherish a just and lasting peace among ourselves, and with all nations.

Douglass was equally moved by Lincoln's words and by the melancholy that shadowed his whole face. Douglass decided to go with Mrs. Dorsey to the inaugural reception that 'evening. He had always been a trailblazer. He felt it was time for the black man to hold up his head among his fellow citizens.

The lights were ablaze in front of the White House when Douglass and Mrs. Dorsey reached the door. Immediately two policemen, who were handling the crowds, stopped him with the explanation, "Our orders are to admit no persons of color."

Douglass was not so easily put off. "I am sure there must be some mistake. President Lincoln cannot possibly have given such an order. If he knew I were here, I'm sure he would want to see me."

Behind Douglass the long line of Lincoln's well-wishers were growing impatient. Douglass stood in the doorway and refused to leave. One of the guards assumed a sickly smile and told Douglass to follow him.

Douglass and Mrs. Dorsey were led through a maze of corridors to a room which turned out to be a temporary exit. A rough bridge of planks led out of the window.

Indignantly Douglass said, "You have deceived me. I shall not go out of this building until you conduct me to Mr. Lincoln."

"Good evening, Douglass," said a voice behind him.

Douglass called after the man, a government official he had once met. "Be so kind as to say to Mr. Lincoln that Frederick Douglass is detained by officers at the door."

Lincoln had given no orders to exclude Douglass. The officers were merely acting on the 'slavery-born assumption of the Negro's inferiority.

Within a few minutes Douglass and Mrs. Dorsey beheld Lincoln "in his grand simplicity and homely beauty" under the blazing chandeliers of the East Room. "Here comes my friend Douglass," Lincoln called.

When Douglass grasped his hand, the president continued. "I am glad to see you. I saw you in the crowd today, listening to my inaugural address. How did you like it?"

"Mr. Lincoln, I must not detain you with my poor opinion, when there are thousands waiting to shake hands with you."

"No, no, you must stop a little, Douglass: there is no man in the country whose opinion I value more than yours. I want to know what you think of it?"

"Mr. Lincoln, that was a sacred effort."

"I am glad you liked it," Lincoln answered as Douglass passed out of his sight.

The end of the war came swiftly. On April 3 Lee abandoned Richmond and the armies of Grant marched in. On April 9 Lee surrendered to Grant at Appomattox courthouse. The Confederates laid down their arms forever.

Rejoicing swept the cities of the North. The South lay dazed, some of her proudest cities in ruins. The remnant of the ragged Confederate army limped home. As word spread to the slaves that "Massa Linkum" had freed them, they took up the chorus of praise.

Then, across all the rejoicings and doubts and fears, cut the horrifying news that Lincoln had been assassinated by a half-crazed Southern actor, John Wilkes Booth. The news reached Douglass at home in Rochester. The following night he joined his grieving fellow citizens at the city hall. Although not scheduled to speak, he gave eloquent tongue to the "agony of the hour." Never had he felt closer to his friends and neighbors than in this hour of national calamity.

Yet, beyond his sadness, Douglass looked hopefully ahead. His people were free at last. With his greatest work crowned by unexpected success, what future tasks would he find for his voice and pen? Douglass suspected his job was by no means done. Unlike some of his simpler friends, he foresaw that "sweet liberty" took more than a piece of paper to win.

16 **a new fight**

I have had but one idea for the last three years to present to the American people, and the phraseology in which I clothe it is the old abolition phraseology. I am for the "immediate, unconditional and universal" enfranchisement of the black man, in every State in the Union.

Frederick Douglass

"No, Mr. Chairman, no; our work is not yet quite done; at least mine is not done, nor will it be done till the blackest man has every right which I, myself, enjoy. I cannot prove I love my neighbor as myself till he stands by my side." Parker Pillsbury, one of the slave's sturdiest defenders in old abolitionist days, was addressing the annual convention of the American Anti-Slavery Society in May 1865. His shaggy brown head was frosted with white, but his voice was as resounding as ever.

All present, including Frederick Douglass, knew that this was one of the most important meetings the society had ever held. Not since the war had so many people attended a convention. All Douglass's old friends were there, some friendly once more, some still cool.

William Lloyd Garrison, in the chair, well expressed the feelings of many of those present. For him victory had been achieved. Therefore, there was no reason to continue the society.

"Today it is popular to be president of the American Anti-Slavery Society," he told the audience. "Hence my connection with it terminates here and now."

Garrison had set out to free the slaves and they were free. Fortunately, many members realized that freedom was not so simple nor so sure a thing. This opposing view was held by Garrison's closest associate—Wendell Phillips. More farseeing

Parker Pillsbury

than his former leader, Phillips had emerged as spokesman for those who wished to continue the society until the Negro had gained his full rights.

When the vote was taken, the motion to continue the society was approved, 118 to 48. Phillips was elected president. Among those who supported him, besides Douglass, were Remond, Purvis, Stephen and Abby Foster, Pillsbury, and the young, high-spirited Anna E. Dickinson.

So Douglass set out to devote his speaking and writing to the cause of Negro suffrage. Like most of the nation, he was still a little numb from the shock of Lincoln's death. Andrew Johnson was an unknown quantity. He was a former governor of Tennessee and before that a poor tailor hostile to the rich Southern planters. Though a Democrat, he had turned Republican through his love of the Union.

Because Johnson was so unfriendly to the Southern

aristocrats, the abolitionists and Radical Republicans in Congress imagined he would be friendly to rights for the ex-slaves. In the summer of 1865 Johnson quickly showed where he stood on this subject. He announced that any Confederate state could organize a government and hold elections when a sufficient number of people there took the oath of allegiance to the Constitution of the United States.

Men like Douglass and Phillips were shocked by this hasty kiss of pardon for the "erring sisters" of the South. In October Douglass told a Baltimore audience that the South would be sure to abuse the power given it.

By the end of 1865 the Southern states had fulfilled Douglass's predictions. They had elected to Congress delegations which included the former vice-president and other high officials of the Confederacy. These men were not even eligible to serve without presidential pardon.

Worse yet, the various Southern states had passed the notorious Black Codes, to control the four million freedmen in their midst. Except for the right to marry, own land, and make contracts, the Negro received almost none of the rights of free men. The provisions regulating his labor were little better than slavery under another name.

As Northern travelers visited the South and reported on the misery of the oppressed ex-slaves, Northern sentiment was aroused. An early sympathy for the defeated South began to give way to anger and revulsion.

In February 1866 a convention of colored men met in Washington. The delegates decided that now was the time to find out where the new president stood on some vital issues. Douglass and George T. Downing, a wealthy Washington restaurateur, were to head a delegation to the White House. Lewis Douglass, who was twenty-five, accompanied his father for the first time.

They were ushered into the presidential office so recently occupied by the Great Emancipator. They found Johnson slouched in a chair, hands in pockets, wearing a rather sour expression. With ill grace he rose to shake hands with each member of the delegation.

The diplomatic Downing opened the interview. He recalled the claims of the black man as native-born American and citizen. Douglass summed up their reasons for coming:

> In the order of Divine Providence you are placed in a position where you have the power to save or destroy us, to bless or blast us—I mean our whole race. Your noble and humane predecessor placed in our hands the sword to assist in saving the nation, and we do hope that you, his able successor, will favorably regard the placing in our hands the ballot with which to save ourselves.

Johnson's face flushed. He seemed angry at the delegation for raising this thorny question. He began to speak in a rambling way, to himself as much as to them. "For the colored race my means, my time, my all has been perilled. . . ." Johnson assured them that he was their true friend, their Moses. But granting the Negro the ballot would start a war between races.

The president talked on for forty-five minutes, waving aside all attempts by Douglass to answer some of his arguments. The main point he kept hitting, like a nail that refused to go in, was the hate and hostility between ex-slave and poor white. His words revealed at once his dislike for Negroes and his resentment of—and admiration for—the cotton-planting aristocrats. The planters had had more contempt for the poor tailor than for their least trusted slaves.

At last Johnson stopped, as if his words had run out. There were mutual expressions of polite thanks.

Douglass managed to say, "You enfranchise your enemies and disfranchise your friends."

As the delegation turned to go, Douglass addressed its members: "The President sends us to the people, and we go to the people."

Anti-black riots like this one in New Orleans in 1866 were one reason Douglass fought so hard to win the vote for his people. (Woodcut)

"Yes, sir," Johnson called after him. "I have great faith in the people. I believe they will do what is right."

The delegation knew that Johnson would publish his views on suffrage for the Negro. Therefore they must do the same. That evening they sent off a reply to the papers in the unmistakable voice of Douglass:

> The hostility between the whites and blacks of the South is easily explained. It has its root and sap in the relation of slavery, and was incited on both sides by the cunning of the slave masters.

With the end of slavery, this hostility would probably disappear unless stirred up again. But even if it didn't, was it fair to leave the black man with no means of defense? Douglass quoted his favorite maxim: "Men are whipped oftenest who are whipped easiest." Degrading the black race would not lead to lasting peace; only equal justice could do that.

Now the battle lines were clearly drawn, the armies face to face in the new battle for Negro rights. On one side was Johnson, the defeated South, and those Northern Democrats who feared the elevation of the black man. On the other side were the Negro leaders, the surviving abolitionists, and the Radical Republicans. They were joined by those Northern conservatives who were disturbed by the South's lack of feeling for the Union.

On September 1, 1866, Douglass was riding south on the familiar train from Rochester. He had just received a most unexpected honor. The people of Rochester had voted him their delegate to a Loyalist convention in Philadelphia. The convention was a political move by the Republicans intended to rally the opponents of Johnson.

At Harrisburg his train was joined to another bringing delegates from the South and West. Douglass smiled at the warm greetings of old friends like generals Butler and Burnside. Not long after, a group of delegates approached his seat. The leader, a gentleman from Louisiana with exquisite Creole manners, gave a slight bow and said:

> Mr. Douglass, I have long known of your history and your works. I myself, as well as the gentlmen who sent me and those who accompany me entertain the highest respect and admiration for you. None among us would have the remotest objection to sitting with you in the convention. Indeed we would count it an honor and a pleasure. But there is a greater good, a common cause which we must consider above our personal wishes. [Author's version of indirect quotation.]

The gentleman from New Orleans explained that, merely from expediency, it might be better if he did not attend the convention. The cry of political equality might damage the party at the polls in the North as well as the South.

Douglass spoke in his most resonant voice: "Gentlemen, with all respect, you might as well ask me to put a loaded pistol to my head and blow my brains out, as to ask me to keep out of this convention, to which I have been duly elected." The charge of cowardice, if they kept him away, might damage their cause more than that of amalgamation (race-mixing). But policy aside, "I am bound to go into that convention; not to do so would contradict the principle and practice of my life."

The delegation bowed itself out of the car.

The next day all the delegates assembled inside the hallowed walls of Independence Hall to begin their march through the streets. Douglass was disappointed but not surprised when no one stopped to shake his hand except General Butler. Even his old friend Senator Henry Wilson of Massachusetts passed by him with only a nod.

By twos the delegates were beginning to file out of the hall into the streets. Still no one had come to Douglass's side nor offered to link arms with him. Well, then, I shall walk alone, he thought.

"Why, Douglass, my friend, just the man I've wanted most to speak to," said a ringing young voice. A welcome hand was laid on Douglass's shoulder. He turned around to see Theodore Tilton, the able and crusading young editor of the New York *Independent*. Here at last was the *one man* whose courage equaled his convictions.

Tilton and Douglass walked arm in arm into the bright September sunshine. Flags were waving from the solid rows of brick-fronted houses. Men, women, and children lined the curbs, cheering the marchers. There was a sudden hush as Douglass drew near. "Here comes Fred Douglass," rang the cry that sent up a roar from the crowd. It was taken up all along the line of march. Douglass had become the hero of the day.

As soon as Douglass had attended the first meeting of the convention, he saw at once how far away was his goal of Negro suffrage. The Northern and Southern delegates could not agree and met separately. The Southern delegates came from states with a large Negro population and favored immediate suffrage. Most of the Northern and border state delegates, except for those from New York, wanted to sweep the appeal for Negro votes under the rug. It was too radical; it was too soon; the elections were coming.

As Douglass watched the convention day by day, he became more and more disappointed with the course of events. There was much criticism of Johnson, but little in the way of solid plans for solving the problems of the freed slaves. On the third night there was a giant rally of Northern and Southern delegates. It was marked by clichés about the glorious Union and the gallant boys in blue. There were torchlight parades, skyrockets and Roman candles, and bands playing the "Battle Hymn of the Republic."

Douglass began to realize that if anyone was to bring up the Negro suffrage amendment, he must act at once. On the fourth morning he and Tilton and Anna Dickinson entered the hall where the Southern delegates were meeting. The border state leaders were trying to maneuver for adjournment before anyone could raise the explosive issue of Negro voting rights. At the sight of the three visitors, the majority of delegates set up loud cheers. Over the gavel of the chairman, they shouted for speeches.

Miss Dickinson stood up. Her piquant beauty drew appreciative glances from the delegates weary of politics. In contrast to her simple gown was the black velvet jockey cap set at a rakish angle on her daringly short dark curls. She swept off the cap, bringing a sharp intake of breath from the fascinated audience. Then she drew out a wisp of linen handkerchief to wipe a brow slightly damp from excitement.

In her silvery voice she told the cautious and hesitant

audience, " . . . there is no backward flow of ideas, more than of rivers. . . . Stepping onward is glory."

Douglass followed with an equally eloquent appeal for the black man's need to vote *now* as his simple right. The border states could no longer smother the delicate question. It was out in the open.

On the last day of the convention the Southern delegates, minus some border state men who walked out, voted to approve a revolutionary report. It demanded that the government "confer on every citizen in the states we represent the American birthright of impartial suffrage and equality before the law."

When Douglass, Tilton, and Miss Dickinson left the hall, they were all a little breathless from the swift flow of events. This public approval of the Negro suffrage report was the opening blast in the campaign which resulted in the passage of the Fifteenth Amendment to the Constitution. This amendment states that:

> The right of citizens of the United States to vote shall not be denied or abridged by the United States or by any State on account of race, color, or previous condition of servitude.

Douglass was to be highly influential in bringing about the final passage of this amendment. In the campaign of 1866 Douglass was asked to take the stump for the Republicans for the first time. The Republicans had made an interesting discovery. The South was returning to its Democratic loyalties and the party was resurgent in the North. So the Republicans needed all the help they could get, even from the slaves they had freed.

Johnson, who now campaigned for the Democrats, helped defeat his own program. He made a "swing around the circle" which was considered demeaning for a president. He drank rather more than was good for him and indulged in vulgar

insults and name-calling with hecklers. The result was a resounding victory for the Republicans.

Now the Radicals proceeded to pass a series of Reconstruction measures for the South over Johnson's veto. The
leaders were Charles Sumner in the Senate and Thaddeus
Stevens in the House. They called for all the Southern states to
pass the Fourteenth Amendment, which guaranteed citizenship and equal rights to Negroes. Union soldiers were to direct
the voting where needed to protect the freedmen.

Douglass and Senator Sumner were happy at these signs
of progress. But both of them had a disquieting and prophetic
understanding of their weakness. No land was given the
freedman; his political power had no economic base to give
it stability. And in America, economic and political power are
inseparable twins.

In July of 1867 Douglass was reminded of the plight of
the ex-slave in a deeply personal way. When he returned home
from a lecture tour, he found in his living room a man with a
scarred face who appeared quite old and bent, a sturdy middle-
aged woman, and five children in their teens. Douglass hesitated. There was a tense and painful silence; then the man
straightened up, giving a much sturdier impression.

Instantly Douglass recognized his brother, Perry, "who
carried me on his shoulders many a time." It was a Perry much
marked by hardship and cruelty. He had been a slave for all
his fifty-six years. He had been sold several times, the end of the
war finding him in Texas. A minister he had met in New
Orleans, on learning he was Douglass's brother, had helped
him on his way to Rochester.

For the rest of the summer Douglass stayed at home.
He devoted himself to Perry, housing him and his family until
"a snug little cottage" was built on his grounds for them. And
there Perry ended his days in peace at last.

But in the fall Douglass returned to the fray. In the presidential campaign of 1868 he helped General Grant win almost

the entire Negro vote of 450,000. Since Grant defeated Sey-
mour by only 300,000 votes, Republicans at last called in
earnest for passage of the Fifteenth Amendment.

Most observers expected Douglass to receive a political
appointment, like minister to Haiti, from the Grant administration. But through a misunderstanding it went to another.

Douglass returned to the lecture hall to lead the final push
for Negro suffrage. This protection was desperately needed by
the freedman in the South. Already such secret organizations as
the Ku Klux Klan, Knights of the White Camelia, and open
semimilitary groups called Red Shirts and the White League,
were active. By threats of violence and actual whippings, club-
bings, lynchings, and shootings in broad daylight, they sought
to terrorize the black man into his prewar submission.

During these years Douglass had to part temporarily from
some old friends. The leaders of the woman's rights movement,
Susan B. Anthony and Elizabeth Cady Stanton, were bitterly
disappointed that women were not included in the Fifteenth
Amendment. Douglass sympathized, but felt the Negro must
have priority because of the constant physical threats which
faced him, especially in the South. Douglass promised that
as soon as the Negro had the vote, he would return to
their banner once more until their cause should be won as
well.

Early in 1869, Congress passed the Fifteenth Amendment
and sent it to the state legislatures. As state by state passed it
through the rest of the year, Douglass could see the star of
victory rising before his eyes. On February 25, 1870, a black
man, Hiram R. Revels of Mississippi, arrived in Washington
to occupy the Senate seat formerly held by Jefferson Davis. On
March 30 Grant announced adoption of the Fifteenth Amendment, "a measure of grander importance than any other act of
the kind from the foundation of our free government to the
present time."

Soon Douglass was caught up in a round of celebrations.

On April 19, 1870, he hurried down Broadway to Apollo
Hall in New York City. It seemed as if every Negro in New
York were parading joyfully around the hall, where the American Anti-Slavery Society was to hold its last meeting. In front
of the door the crowds parted and held up torches to light a
path for the heroes of the struggle.

Douglass was cheered all the way to the platform. Almost
all the living members were there—Lucretia Mott, Robert
Purvis, Julia Ward Howe, Abby Kelley Foster, Henry Highland
Garnet, and, of course, Wendell Phillips in the chair. Only
Garrison held aloof.

Douglass sat next to his old friends, reflecting on the in-
credible events of the last twenty-nine years. All bitterness that
had once divided them was swallowed up in his joy and sense
of indebtedness. Suppose Garrison had never heard him speak
on Nantucket? Suppose he had never received his education
from men and women like Phillips, May, Mrs. Mott, the
Fosters, and, of course, Garrison himself? Would he ever have
been more than a New Bedford laborer of some intelligence
with a taste for Sunday preaching and teaching?

Douglass spoke, with his old plague of hoarseness render-
ing his words yet more poignant:

> I seem to myself to be living in a new world. The sun
> does not shine as it used to. . . . Not only the slave emanci-
> pated, but a personal liberty bill, a civil rights bill, ad-
> mitted to give testimony in courts of justice, given the
> right to vote, eligible not only to Congress, but the Presi-
> dential chair—and all for a class stigmatized but a little
> while ago as worthless goods and chattels.

Douglass's voice broke several times as he thanked God
and those faithful men and women who had realized this great
advance in the "welfare of mankind."

He ended with a warm glance that tried to take in every delegate in the hall:

> I don't want to part from you at all; and I am glad to know that we are to unite in other works, and that though the form of this association shall be dissolved, the spirit which animates it . . . is to continue its activity through new instrumentalities, for the Indian whose condition to-day is the saddest chapter of our history. . . . And our energies are not only to be devoted to this, but to the interests of suffering humanity everywhere; and for woman, too, for whose cause we can now labor upon a common platform.

As the last moments of this great human effort drew near, Wendell Phillips rose to deliver his brief valedictory:

> And so, friends, we will not say, "Farewell," but we will say, "All hail, welcome to new duties." We sheathe no sword. We only turn from the front rank of the army upon a new foe.

Douglass had discharged his debt of gratitude to those who had helped in the fight. But his part was not forgotten. Letters poured in from men and women of his race, expressing pride and joy in the crowning of his labors with victory. The greatest tribute came at a giant celebration in Baltimore on May 19. It read:

> Resolved, That recognizing in Frederick Douglass the foremost man of color in the times in which we live, and proud to claim him as one "to the manor born," we do here most respectfully, yet earnestly, request him to return to us, and by the power of his magnificent manhood help us to a higher, broader, and nobler manhood.

17 **honor and heartbreak**

*There is one thing, however, in which I think we must all agree at
the start. It is that this so-called but mis-called Negro problem is one
of the most important and urgent subjects that can now engage
public attention.*

Frederick Douglass

It was a golden autumn day in 1880. A carriage rattled across
the Anacostia Bridge spanning the Anacostia branch of the
Potomac River in Washington. It entered the gates of an ex-
tensive wooded estate and wound halfway up a steep hill past
peacefully grazing cows to a circular drive, where it stopped.
Out stepped Elizabeth Chace, now past seventy, and her
daughter Lillie (Mrs. Arthur Wyman), come to see Frederick
Douglass in his new Washington home, Cedar Hill.

They were facing the side of a large, imposing brick-
fronted house, which was half hidden by the dark green spikes
of the cedars. Slowly they walked up a long flight of stone steps
and came around to the front porch, the roof of which was supported by four pillars. For a moment they looked down the hill
and over the roofs of the new row houses below to the windings
of the Potomac. Then they knocked on the door.

They were shown in by the housekeeper, Louisa Sprague,
the sister of Rosetta's husband, Nathan. As they passed
through the carpeted hall, they were greeted by portraits of old
friends like Garrison, Phillips, Susan B. Anthony, and Elizabeth
Cady Stanton, as well as Lincoln.

Douglass rose to greet them in the larger parlor, one of the
twenty spacious rooms in the house. They looked in on Anna,
in her smaller parlor across the hall. Since she suffered from
ever-worsening arthritis, she nodded and smiled from her chair.

Douglass's first Washington home (he may be the man at right), now the Frederick Douglass Institute of Negro Arts and Letters

Douglass had occupied Cedar Hill since shortly after his appointment to his first political office as Marshal of the District of Columbia three years earlier. Here he could hold open house for his children and grandchildren. Lewis and Amelia, a devoted couple, had remained childless. However, Fred Jr., Charles, and Rosetta each had seven children, whom their grandfather loved to entertain.

Before they settled down to talk, Douglass showed Mrs. Chace and Mrs. Wyman his favorite room—the upstairs study —the walls of which were lined with two thousand books. Now that he was marshal, he need no longer spend six months of the year on the lecture circuit to make a living. He had leisure to read and study as he had longed to do in his difficult and demanding youth.

As they took their tea in the parlor, Douglass told his guests that he had bought the house from a once-rich landowner who had built it for his own use. When rich, this man had always refused to sell land to Negroes or Irishmen. But after losing his money in the panic of 1873, he had been willing to sell the house to whoever could pay for it.

Mrs. Chace congratulated Douglass on his high position. She remarked on how far he had advanced since he had warmed himself at her kitchen fire as a fugitive slave and much-abused anti-slavery agent.

"Oh, we have come far, very far, I am hopeful, despite recent setbacks. I remember once long ago Gerrit Smith of blessed memory told me that 'your mission, Douglass, is to break down the walls of separation between the two races.' So I feel that in accepting the Marshal's job, I made an advance since I was the first of my race to receive it."

Mrs. Chace said no more on a subject that Douglass's friends so often discussed. Frederick Douglass's abilities should have earned him a higher office than he had yet held. When his old friend, the Reverend Samuel J. May, wrote his *Reminiscences* in 1869, he had assumed that Douglass would soon be elected to Congress. This hope was not fullfilled.

Douglass did not feel it right to establish residence in a Southern district with a high Negro population just in order to be elected to Congress. During the Reconstruction period, from 1869 to 1876, fourteen Negroes from the South sat in the House of Representatives, and two in the Senate. But Douglass was never elected to any office except the honorary one of presidential elector from New York in 1872.

Perhaps the knowledge that the anti-slavery North was not ready to send him to Congress helped persuade Douglass to

move to Washington. There were other reasons—as the recognized black leader, he could best represent his people and
speak for their rights in the national capital. Then too he
knew Anna would be happier there. Washington had a black
population of forty thousand against the two hundred left in
Rochester.

Douglass told Mrs. Chace of the disaster which had helped
strengthen his decision to leave Rochester. In the early summer
of 1872 Douglass had been on a lecture tour. On June 2 he received a wire giving the sad news that the house on South
Avenue had burned to the ground. Fortunately, Anna, Rosetta, and her husband and children had escaped, but his furniture, library, and the complete files of his paper had been
burned.

Douglass reached Rochester at one o'clock in the morning in a downpour. Not wishing to arouse his friends at that
hour to find out where his family was staying, he hurried to
the nearest hotel. The hesitating and embarrassed manner of
the desk clerk when he asked for a room was a surprise and a
disappointment.

Still, half hoping his impression was wrong, he went across
the street to the Waverly House. Again his query met the
shifting eyes, the shaking of the averted head.

Douglass turned to leave in disgust when a voice called
him. "Oh, Mr. Douglass, I'm afraid there's been a mistake.
Of course, we can accommodate *you.*"

Douglass turned around and saw that the hotel manager
was addressing him. "Blockhead," said the manager to his
clerk, "can't you recognize Mr. Douglass when you see him?"

"I'm afraid I cannot accept your offer of a room," said
Douglass in a very chilly tone. "I prefer to find out where my
family is staying and join them. My appearance, except for one
small detail, was no less respectable when your clerk did not
know me."

Douglass was discouraged. He had lived twenty-five years

in the liberal Northern city of Rochester. Yet he could not find a room for the night at the local hotel unless he was known to be a person of importance.

For a few moments Douglass talked to Mrs. Chace of the discouragement he sometimes felt at the rise of the "Ku Klux spirit," North as well as South. In fact, he owed his position as marshal in part to the Compromise of 1876, which had killed Reconstruction in the South.

The election between Rutherford B. Hayes, the Republican, and Samuel J. Tilden, the Democrat, had been so close that Congress had had to appoint an electoral commission to decide it. In the final "deal," the Republicans were given the election in return for the withdrawal of federal troops from the South.

This withdrawal of troops left the Negro voters in the South without protection. Those black voters who were not willing to support the Democratic ticket were either terrorized into submission, lynched, or shot. So when Douglass had accepted the office of marshal after such a defeat for his people, he had been severely criticized. Many Negroes denounced the appointment as appeasement.

Douglass did not regard his job in that light. He felt he could do his people more good in the government than out of it. Soon after taking office he stirred up a hornet's nest by attacking segregation in the District of Columbia. And he had publicly criticized Hayes for withdrawing the troops.

In office or out, his principle was the same:

> When the influence of office, or any other influence, shall soften my hatred of tyranny and violence, do not spare me, let fall upon me the lash of your keenest and most withering censure.

Douglass and Mrs. Chace were silent for a moment, both thinking, perhaps, of how far the black man had still to travel to gain equality. Then Douglass tried to divert her with a more personal story.

"Enough of politics," he said. "I imagine you would like to hear the true story of my meeting with my old master Thomas Auld in Saint Michaels."

Douglass explained that he had gone to St. Michaels at the invitation of his old friend Charles Caldwell. Once there, he had received word that Captain Auld, who was lying on his deathbed, wished to see him. It was a strange sensation for Douglass to come up the path to the house where he had suffered so much. But his heart had been softened toward Captain Auld by the knowledge that he had cared for Grandmama Betsy in her weakness and old age.

Captain Auld lay on his bed, supported by pillows. Even so his head drooped dangerously, shaking slightly from palsy. He and Douglass looked at each other. As they did, that flash of sympathy passed between them that the system of slavery had always repressed. Each greeted the other simultaneously. "Marshal Douglass!" "Captain Auld!"

Douglass came up to the bed, grasped Auld's hand, and said, "Not *Marshal*, but Frederick to you as formerly." These words drew forth from his old master's eyes the easy tears of weakness.

Douglass's spontaneous gesture had put them both at ease. They talked freely, for Captain Auld's mind had remained clear, despite his suffering. Douglass asked him what he had thought when he heard that Douglass had run away to the North.

Captain Auld answered, "I always knew you were too smart to be a slave, Frederick. And had I been in your place, I would have done as you did."

Douglass spoke soothingly. "Captain Auld, I am glad to hear you say that. I did not run away from *you*, but from *slavery*."

Then they talked of Grandmama Betsy's last days. Captain Auld said suddenly, "Oh, I never liked slavery, and meant to emancipate all my slaves when they reached twenty-five." Douglass said he felt they had both been victims of a system.

Captain Auld began to stare fixedly at the rays of the sun coming in between the slats in the shutters. He spoke "with full confidence of the great change that awaited him, and felt himself about to depart in peace." Douglass had been in the room but twenty minutes when he bade the captain goodbye. He felt his old master was already half in the other world. Soon after, he read of Thomas Auld's death. The newspapers were mostly interested in the fact that Douglass had once been his slave.

Shortly after telling Mrs. Chace and Mrs. Wyman this story, Douglass escorted them back to Mrs. Wyman's house in his own carriage. Mrs. Chace later wrote an account of her visit for the *Providence Journal*:

> As a kingly man, as a high-bred gentleman, no man in this broad land stands before Frederick Douglass. Looking at him as he stands scholarly broad in every sense . . . large-hearted, philanthropic, with lofty aims and unselfish ambitions, crowned with honors he had fairly won, in spite of all these drawbacks [early suffering, lack of education, color] and modestly ignoring all greater honors, that, but for the one dishonor of race might now be his, what other man, in this or any other land, has a right to call himself his peer?

At the time of Mrs. Chace's visit, Frederick Douglass was about 63. He had reached the age when many men begin to plan their retirement from public life and office. It is an age when those who have gained some wealth and power are likely to grow conservative. Even those who have been progressive in their youth are likely to view the strivings of the young men of a later age without sympathy.

There were moments when it seemed that Frederick

Helen Pitts Douglass

Douglass had become such a conservative, older man. His material comfort cut him off from the daily struggles of the poverty-stricken masses of Negroes, most of whom were landless laborers in the South.

However, when Douglass became aware of an injustice, he denounced it. This was why he maintained a remarkable hold on the affections of the black community to the end of his life. One black editor summed up his power thus: "Frederick Douglass was the only Negro who spoke in season and out for his race."

At this time Douglass was absorbed in family affairs and his Washington office. In the summer of 1882 Anna, long disabled, suffered a stroke. Within four weeks, despite devoted nursing, she died.

Douglass, at sixty-five, began to feel old. He wrote Susan

B. Anthony that "Mother was the post in the center of my house."

On a January evening in 1884 a carriage drew up before the home of the Reverend Francis J. Grimké, a young and brilliant Negro Presbyterian minister. Four people got out and were shown into his living room. They were Blanche K. Bruce, former black senator from Mississippi, Mrs. Bruce, Frederick Douglass, and a white woman named Helen Pitts. Miss Pitts was a forty-six-year-old graduate of Mount Holyoke College. A native of Rochester, she had served as Douglass's secretary in his Washington office.

Grimké performed a simple wedding ceremony for Douglass and Miss Pitts, and the couple left for Cedar Hill. Grimké always remembered how "radiant and happy" they both looked.

Within two hours the news had leaked to the newspapers. Immediately, a cloudburst of criticism descended on the couple from both whites and blacks. Some Negroes thought Douglass was showing contempt for the women of his own race; others thought that Helen wasn't good enough for him. Many whites denounced the marriage on the grounds of the supposed inferiority of the darker races.

Douglass and Helen were well matched in their interests and strong in their mutual love. Helen said simply, "Love came to me and I was not afraid to marry the man I loved because of his color."

Douglass would sometimes quip, "It merely proves I am quite impartial. My first wife was the color of my mother, and my second is the color of my father."

Several months later Douglass explained more seriously the philosophy that had always guided him: "I base no man's right upon his color and plead no man's rights because of his color. . . . My sympathies are not limited by my relation to any race."

Though some of his people were shocked by his marriage, Douglass never lost their love and affection because of it. And his best friends, black and white, wrote sincere congratulations at his happiness.

The visitor to Cedar Hill after Douglass's second marriage immediately felt the deep, quiet content that radiated from the master and mistress of the house. In summer they might join Douglass and Helen for a game of croquet on the lawn. At afternoon tea famous guests mingled with students from nearby Howard University. In the evenings Helen would sit down at the piano to accompany Douglass as he played his favorite Scottish airs on the violin.

Young Negroes came from far and near to discuss personal, professional, and race problems with Douglass. Among his protégés was the promising young poet, Paul Laurence Dunbar. The rising young civil rights leader, Mary Church Terrell, was a frequent visitor with her distinguished husband, Judge Robert Terrell. She was one of those who would carry Douglass's fight for equality into the next generation.

In 1886-87 Douglass took Helen on a long-dreamed-of tour of England, France, Italy, Greece, and Egypt. He met old friends and made new ones.

When Douglass returned to America, the politicians were already looking forward to the election of 1888. Douglass had campaigned for the Republicans in every national election since 1866. He felt the party of Lincoln, whatever its faults, had more to offer the Negro than the Democrats, the party of the Southern planters.

Douglass had been hearing disquieting rumors of the condition of the freedmen. In the spring of 1888 he made a tour of South Carolina and Georgia. He was immeasurably shocked by what he saw. The freedmen were once again at the mercy of their former masters. They were cheated of their wages and tricked out of their votes. He realized how little he had understood of their wretchedness. All his old fight rekindled.

The lost champions—Stevens, Sumner, Garrison, Garnet,

and Phillips—who had once raised their voices with his were replaced by men who marched to the beat of a different drum. The great wave of reform and religious enthusiasm, which had given birth to abolitionism and freed the slave, had diminished. Reformers of the new generation wanted to clean up the corruption of the Grant era, remove the patronage from the civil service, or overhaul the country's monetary and tariff laws. They had no interest in the Negro. He was a citizen now, wasn't he? Let him fend for himself.

Many of these new reformers had tasted the same racist brew as their Southern brothers. When they looked at the poor, ignorant workers flooding American cities from Eastern and Central Europe, they began to sympathize with the South about the superiority of the Anglo-Saxon race. To them the Poles, Italians, Czechs, Greeks, Russians, and Jews were scarcely better than blacks. All were "corrupting the purity" of native Americans.

In this discouraging atmosphere even many Negroes began to counsel silent acquiescence to terror, but not Douglass. He rose to address the twenty-sixth anniversary celebration of emancipation in the District of Columbia. His voice swelled with the power of his prime, now solemn as an organ, now quivering with righteous indignation.

He wished to answer those who asked why the Negro on the plantation had made so little progress. He described the terrible conditions he had seen.

> I ask, in view of it all, how, in the name of human reason, could the Negro be expected to rise higher in the scale of morals, manners, religion and civilization than he has during the twenty years of his freedom? Shame,

Mr. and Mrs. Frederick Douglass at home in Cedar Hill. The young woman standing has been identified as Helen's sister, Eva Pitts.

eternal shame, on those writers and speakers who taunt, denounce, and disparage the Negro because he is to-day found in poverty, rags and wretchedness.

Finally Douglass pointed a finger of accusation at the national government, which imposed on the Negro the burdens of citizenship—taxes, war service—without granting him its blessings and protection.

As the voice of the old Douglass rang through the land, Negroes from all over the country poured in messages of their gratitude for his forthright stand. The disfranchised of the South wrote to him of how well he had understood their desperate situation.

In June Douglass went before the Republican convention and spoke in the same passionate vein. He called for "no more fooling, no more hazing, no more humbug, no more keeping the promise to the ear and breaking it to the heart."

The party platform came out for stronger federal protection of the rights of Negroes. On this plank Douglass campaigned vigorously for Benjamin Harrison. When Harrison won, he attended the inaugural reception with John Hutchinson, the sweet singer of abolition days, still going strong despite his white hair.

Douglass was surprised and pleased when Harrison appointed him minister to Haiti, the highest post he had ever held. Many of his friends criticized the appointment. Some said it was not big enough for him. Others feared the hot climate would be bad for his health. Still others thought the government wanted to get him out of the way so he could no longer expose the condition of the Southern Negro.

Douglass, however, was happy to visit the black republic at last. He felt American Negroes owed a debt of gratitude to the first nation of former slaves to gain freedom. He was welcomed with greatest honor by President Hippolyte and the Haitian people.

Douglass served with distinction for two years. In 1891 he resigned, partly for reasons of health. The Haitians deeply regretted his going. American Negroes were glad to have him back. An admirer from the South wrote:

> We miss you very much indeed. In whatever direction I look the tide seems to be setting in strongly against us and there is not a single man in the country able to stem it or turn it or break its force. You are needed here.

The America to which the much-aged Douglass returned in 1891 was suffering from an increasingly split personality in relation to him and his race. For Douglass the man there were honors and praise. He was asked to dedicate monuments and lead memorial celebrations by governors, mayors, and college presidents. Universities conferred honorary degrees upon the man who had never spent a day in formal school. Friends asked his influence in securing government employment.

In looking back on his long journey from a Maryland slave cabin, Douglass could truly say, "I have fought the good fight." In his lifelong struggle on behalf of his people, he had been unsparing of himself—mentally and physically. Much had been accomplished—slavery was abolished and the citizenship and voting rights of Negroes were written into the Constitution. No man had done more to achieve these great ends than Frederick Douglass.

Men in their middle and late seventies are not expected to start new movements and lead revolutions. Yet, looked at objectively in the early 1890s, what had the Negro achieved? How far had he progressed?

Never since the end of the war had the Negro been more degraded, dishonored, disfranchised, and physically threatened with torture and death than he was now in the South. A new economic bondage made him little better than a slave. By clever legal dodges he was systematically deprived of his vote.

Perhaps mercifully, Douglass was not to live to see the full malign flowering of the whole elaborate structure of Jim Crow. But he did see the beginning and steady rise of the most horrible and spectacular weapon of terror—lynching, often on the unproved accusation of attacking a white woman or child. (But not always—sometimes it was the old cry of "insolence" or striking a white man.)

During the last sixteen years of the nineteenth century twenty-five hundred Negroes were lynched, many by the incredibly barbaric method of burning alive. Nor did the practice die out with the new century. Douglass could not decide which horrified him more—the fiendish cruelty of the mob, or the almost universal tendency, North as well as South, somehow to transfer the blame from the oppressors to their victims. Even Northern friends of the Negro, and some black leaders, advised silence.

But Douglass was not to be silenced. He sensed that now, as never before, his people needed a champion whose authority and integrity were unquestioned. What to him were the honors and tributes if his life's work was to be so ruthlessly destroyed?

With the righteous wrath of a prophet he composed his last great defense of his people against all the false charges used to excuse the crimes against them. The wisdom, insight, and iron logic of his maturer years united with the thundering denunciations of evil that had once lifted audiences from their seats. The result was an article in the *A.M.E. Review* of July 1894, called "The Lesson of the Hour," later made into a pamphlet.

"Not a breeze comes to us," he began, "from the late rebellious states that is not tainted and freighted with Negro blood." The mob had replaced the sheriffs, constables, and police. Morever the leaders of society were as much to blame as the ignorant mob. Instead of condemning the lynchers, these leaders simply excused their crimes.

And who, after all, Douglass continued, are the men who

accuse the black man of these crimes? They are the same men who openly resort to every kind of trick to cheat the Negro of his vote. Why then believe their latest charge? Isn't it significant that they don't allow the accused time to testify in his own defense before rushing him to the gallows?

This charge of assaulting white women was merely the latest device to keep the Negro in his "place." Before the war blacks were persecuted to control "Negro insurrections." During Reconstruction thousands of blacks were terrorized and killed to prevent them from voting on the cry that their votes would lead to "Negro supremacy." No one believes in Negro insurrection or Negro supremacy any more. So the South has come up with a new charge of "Negro criminality."

The stereotype of the Negro as a comic and degraded figure was undermining his position in the country as a whole. The whole race was slighted at the Columbian Exposition of 1893, which included no exhibit of Negro contributions to America. This omission announced to the world "that the colored people of America are not deemed by Americans as within the compass of American law, progress and civilization." It says to the mobs of the South, "You kill their bodies, we kill their souls."

Douglass had long hoped that America was "too just and magnanimous to oppress the weak." But he was growing doubtful. The future looked so stormy and troubled that he could only hope all would come right in the end.

"He is a wiser man than I am," continued Douglass, "who can tell how low the moral sentiment of the Republic may yet fall." Important safeguards to liberty and justice had been swept away; the civil rights bill was inoperative in the face of states' rights. The Republican party is "converted into a party of money, rather than a party of humanity and justice. . . . The cause lost in the war is the cause regained in the peace."

Then in stirring and prophetic words, Douglass summed up his conclusions:

Now the real problem is, and ought to be regarded by the American people as, a great national problem. It involves the question whether after all our boasted civilization, our Declaration of Independence, our matchless Constitution, our sublime Christianity, our wise statesmanship, we as a people, possess virtue enough to solve this problem in accordance with wisdom and justice. . . .

But my friends, I must stop. Time and strength are not equal to the task before me. But could I be heard by this great nation, I would call to mind the sublime and glorious truths with which, at its birth, it saluted and startled a listening world. . . . Apply these sublime and glorious truths to the situation now before you. Put away your race prejudice. Banish the idea that one class must rule over another. Recognize the fact that the rights of the humblest citizens are as worthy of protection as are those of the highest . . . [and] your Republic will stand and flourish forever.

And with these words Frederick Douglass rested his case with history.

18 in the trade winds of god

It was not because he advanced the interests of the Negro that men will honor his memory today, but because, by advancing the interest of the Negro, he raised the level of all manhood and made the world better by living in it.

The Brooklyn Eagle, February 21, 1895

On the afternoon of February 20, 1895, the door of Metzerott Hall in Washington, D.C., swung open. The annual convention of the National Council of Women was in session. But when she saw the distinguished visitor at the door, Mary Wright Sewall, the chairman, suspended the business under discussion.

A tall, broad-shouldered man of dignified carriage, yellow bronze skin, piercing brown eyes, and impressive features came slowly down the aisle. Though his hair and beard were totally white, he was only slightly stooped with age. Two white women, one almost as old as he, escorted him to the platform. The older woman had snow-white hair and was thin and somewhat bent, but she walked with a light step. The man was Frederick Douglass and the older woman was Susan B. Anthony.

As Douglass passed them, the women rose in row after row, waving their white linen handkerchiefs in greeting. Douglass gave a brief, much-applauded address. His voice was not as strong as of old, but its deeper reverberations had mellowed. From years of practice, its carrying power remained.

Douglass reminded them of his long attachment to the cause of woman's rights. Few remained who had, like him, attended the pioneer Woman's Rights Convention at Seneca Falls, New York, almost fifty years before. He always remembered and was grateful for the role women had played in the

The Frederick Douglass National Memorial, Cedar Hill, in Anacostia, Washington, D.C. Funds are being sought to restore the estate.

fight against slavery. To him, the fight for woman suffrage was the same struggle for greater human freedom in a slightly different guise.

February 20 was a typical day in Douglass's life in his later years. After supper he was scheduled to deliver a lecture at the Hillsdale African Church near Cedar Hill.

He returned home to eat supper with Helen after the meeting. When they had finished eating they sat down in the living room to wait for the carriage which was to take Douglass

to his evening's appointment at 7:00 p.m. Having a few minutes
to spare, he began to describe the afternoon's meeting to Helen.
He rose to illustrate a point. Then he sank to his knees. Helen
watched with interest, thinking he was dramatizing the words
of one of the speakers. She always enjoyed his graphic way of
telling a story.

Douglass said not a word; his head sank lower and lower
till he was completely crumpled up on the floor. Helen's
expression changed from puzzlement to blank despair. For a
moment she sat frozen.

At last recovering the use of her limbs, she rushed for
help. But it was too late. He died easily, painlessly, without
regaining consciousness, just as the carriage rolled up to drive
him to his evening lecture.

The word was flashed to the nation and the world that
the greatest leader of black America had died. The women
whom Douglass had so recently addressed heard it as they
were opening their evening meeting. They immediately
adopted a memorial, which was typical of those that filled the
liberal Northern newspapers and poured into Cedar Hill in
the days that followed. They remarked that it was indeed a "historic coincidence that the man who, in his own person, em-
bodied the history of almost a century, in the struggle between
freedom and oppression, should spend his last day as a witness
of the united efforts . . ." of another disfranchised group to
gain greater freedom.

> Born a slave, his human instinct drove him early to
> forge his way to freedom. Liberty secured, his robust man-
> hood made for himself an heroic career of service to his
> kindred, to his race, to his country and to the world. The
> tenderness of a refined nature sweetened his family life
> and ennobled his friendships. In the army of progress he
> was the trusted comrade and the respected leader of men
> and women living and dead, whom the years more and
> more will understand and honor. . . .

From at home and abroad came messages of praise and regret from societies and organizations devoted to the furthering of human freedom. The Fusion legislature of North Carolina adjourned for the day. The state legislatures of Massachusetts, New York, Indiana, and Illinois passed memorial tributes. That of Illinois recognized him as

> one of the leaders of the world's thought . . . he contributed largely to the final overthrow of the slave system in the United States and the enlargement of the theories and practices of a free government and the liberties of all its citizens . . . .

Most of all from Negroes, individually and in concert, North and South, came a tidal outpouring of grief and praise. The sense of having lost someone irreplaceable ran through their moving messages. The black citizens of Americus, Georgia, in the midst of their poverty and oppression, composed a resolution which lamented that "Frederick Douglass, our Moses, has been taken by God." Then they detailed all their sufferings and Douglass's brilliant, lifelong appeals to the "Christian conscience of the North, the nation and the world, to liberate his people." Yet they ended on a note of hope:

> No people who can produce a Douglass need despair. His life, his struggles, and his achievements shall be the standard of our race and through their inspiration it shall rise.

On the morning of February 25, long lines of black men, women, and children were waiting before the doors of the Metropolitan African Methodist Episcopal Church in Washington. All were silent and some were weeping. Then the lines parted. Heads were uncovered and bowed. A massive oak coffin was borne through the door by a black division of the Sons of Veterans, who formed the guard of honor.

A brief scripture reading and prayer had been Douglass's good-bye at Cedar Hill. Now the whole black community of Washington walked slowly, solemnly past the coffin to say good-bye to the still face of their fallen leader. The Negro children had been let out of school and filed past with their teachers. Delegations had come from the chief cities of the Eastern Seaboard.

At 1:30 the doors of the church were closed for the solemn service. Chief among the Negro notables who delivered eulogies was Oxford scholar Alexander Crummell, the last survivor of that distinguished school class of New York City leaders that had included Ward and Garnet. Susan B. Anthony delivered another address. The most distinguished government representative present was, fittingly, Justice John Marshall Harlan. The next year he was to deliver the sole and stinging dissent to the famous Supreme Court decision condoning "separate but equal" schools that was to stand for almost sixty years.

After the speeches and the prayers, John Hutchinson rose. His voice had remained strong and true. Despite his deep emotion he sang without a tremor the words that his brother Jesse had written in honor of Douglass more than fifty years before:

> I'll be free, I'll be free, and none shall confine
> With fetters and chains this spirit of mine;
> From my youth I have vowed in God to rely,
> And, despite the oppressor, gain freedom or die.

Then he followed more softly with "Lay Him Low."

Two hours later Helen Douglass, with the three living Douglass children—Rosetta, Charles, and Lewis—sat on the train heading North. Frederick Douglass was taking his last trip to Rochester.

The city was in mourning on February 26 for the return of

its great citizen. Flags flew at half mast; school children were let out to file past the body lying in state in city hall. In mid-afternoon, old friends and prominent citizens of Rochester, including the mayor and the board of aldermen, gathered in Central Presbyterian Church. Another solemn service paid respectful tribute to "one of Rochester's most honored and representative men."

A pale late-afternoon sun was still casting its light on the snow when the church doors opened. Slowly the procession moved out. Crowds lined the streets all the way to the cemetery as the hearse, draped in black crepe, bore the coffin up the hill to Mount Hope Cemetery. With muffled drums the bands played a dead march. Then, at the gates of the wooded cemetery, the bands stopped.

Only the carriages bearing close friends and family wound around the snowy paths to the beautiful plot where Anna Douglass and little Annie already slept. The trees were gaunt and bare in the fading light. As the sun sank, their shadows grew purple, then navy blue, on the snow. With a few simple prayers the family said their last good-bye.

So Frederick Douglass rested in death. He had accomplished so much, and so much he had accomplished seemed already destroyed. Throughout the land, for his people, it was winter, it was night.

Yet in a way his ideas were like the maple buds, tightly sheltering their new life from the February cold. Throughout the long years of silence and agonizingly slow progress, they would nourish a few brave hearts.

Then, under a more fiery sun seventy years later, those ideas would burst forth again with an impact that would seem

Frederick Douglass Monument in Rochester, New York, unveiled on September 14, 1898. Governor Theodore Roosevelt was present.

totally modern. Once again the question of Frederick Douglass would be posed to the country that had refused to answer him long ago—the hard, basic, inescapable question:

> Whether American justice, American liberty, American civilization, American law and American Christianity could be made to include and protect alike and forever all American citizens in the rights which have been guaranteed to them by the organic and fundamental laws of the land.

A.M.E. Review, October 1889

bibliography

Basic to the study of Frederick Douglass are his three autobiographies, which are the only direct sources for his early life. The copies of Douglass's best known speeches, found in the research collections of the New York Public Library, supplement the forty file boxes of Douglass speeches, letters, papers, clippings, memorabilia, and photographs preserved in Washington, D.C., by the National Capital Parks Department of the National Park Service. This department is now administering and planning the restoration of the Douglass home. In addition, any student of Douglass is indebted to the scholarly research of Professors Benjamin Quarles and Philip Foner.

The chief works on Douglass, some out of print, are:

Chesnutt, Charles W. *Frederick Douglass*. Boston, 1899.
Douglass, Frederick. *Narrative of the Life of Frederick Douglass, an American Slave*. Boston, 1845.
————. *Life and Times of Frederick Douglass*. Boston, 1892.
————. *My Bondage and My Freedom*. Rochester, 1855.
Foner, Philip S. *The Life and Writings of Frederick Douglass*. 4 vols. New York, 1950-55.
Graham, Shirley. *There Was Once a Slave: The Heroic Story of Frederick Douglass*. New York, 1947.
Holland, Frederick May. *Frederick Douglass*. New York, 1891.
Quarles, Benjamin. *Frederick Douglass*. New York, 1968.
Thompson, John W. *An Authentic History of the Douglass Monument*. Rochester, 1903.
Washington, Booker T. *Frederick Douglass*. 1907.

CONTEMPORARY PAMPHLETS AND POLEMICAL WORKS

American Anti-Slavery Society. *American Slavery as It Is*. New York, 1839.
Bingham, Caleb. *The Columbian Orator*. Boston, 1807.
Carey, John L. *Slavery in Maryland*. Baltimore, 1835.
Douglass, Frederick. Various speeches, 1846-92. *Lessons of the Hour*. Washington, D.C., 1894.
Griffiths, Julia, ed. *Autographs for Freedom*. Boston, 1853.
————. *Autographs for Freedom*. Rochester, 1854.
Miller, Kelly. "Radicals and Conservatives." *Race Adjustment*. New York, 1908.
————. "Frederick Douglass." *The Everlasting Stain*. New York, 1924.
Proceedings of the Colored National Convention Held in Rochester, N.Y., July 6, 7, 8, 1853. Rochester, 1853.

ARTICLES AND ESSAYS

Brewer, W. M. "Henry Highland Garnet." *Journal of Negro History* 13 (1928).

Grimké, Francis J. "The Second Marriage of Frederick Douglass." *Journal of Negro History* 19 (1934).

Hamner-Croughton, Amy. "Anti-Slavery Days in Rochester." Rochester Historical Society *Publications* 14 (1936).

Holland, Frederick May. "Frederick Douglass." *Open Court*. March 1895.

"The Lloyds of 'Wye House,' Talbot County, Maryland." *Maryland Original Research Society Bulletin* 1, Baltimore (1906).

McGuire, Horace. "Two Episodes of Anti-Slavery Days." Rochester Historical Society *Publications* 4 (1925).

Parker, Jane Marsh. "Reminiscences of Frederick Douglass." *The Outlook*, 6 April 1895.

Porter, Dorothy B. "David Ruggles, An Apostle of Human Rights." *Journal of Negro History*, January 1943.

Quarles, Benjamin. "The Breach Between Douglass and Garrison." *Journal of Negro History*, April 1938.

————. "Frederick Douglass and John Brown." Rochester Historical Society *Publications* 17 (1939).

Sprague, Rosetta Douglass. "Anna Murray Douglass—My Mother as I Recall Her." *Journal of Negro History*, January 1923.

Stanton, Theodore. "Frederick Douglass in Paris." *Open Court*. April 1887.

CONTEMPORARY PERIODICALS

Douglass' Monthly. Rochester, 1859-63.
Frederick Douglass' Paper. Rochester, 1851-55.
The Liberator. Boston, 1831-65.
The National Anti-Slavery Standard. New York, 1840-70.
The North Star. Rochester, 1847-51.

HISTORICAL AND GENERAL BACKGROUND

Aptheker, Herbert, ed. *Documentary History of the Negro People in the United States*. New York, 1951.

Botkin, B. A., ed. *Lay My Burden Down*. Chicago, 1945.

Brackett, Jeffrey R. *The Negro in Maryland*. Baltimore, 1889.

Buckmaster, Henrietta. *Let My People Go*: Boston, 1959.

Du Bois, W. E. B. *Black Reconstruction in America*. Cleveland, 1962.

Dumond, Dwight Lowell. *Antislavery: The Crusade for Freedom in America*. Ann Arbor, 1961.

Elkins, Stanley. *Slavery, A Problem in American Institutional and Intellectual Life*. New York, 1963.

Emilio, Luis F. *History of the Fifty-Fourth Regiment of the Massachusetts Volunteer Infantry, 1863-65*. Boston, 1891.

Filler, Louis. *The Crusade Against Slavery, 1830-1860*. New York, 1960.

Footner, Hulbert. *Rivers of the Eastern Shore*. New York, 1944.

Franklin, John Hope. *The Emancipation Proclamation*. New York, 1963.

————. *From Slavery to Freedom, A History of Negro Americans*. New York, 1967.

————. *Reconstruction: After the Civil War*. Chicago, 1961.
Jenkins, William Sumner. *Pro-Slavery Thought in the Old South*. Magnolia, Mass., 1959.
Litwack, Leon F. *North of Slavery: The Negro in the Free States, 1790-1860*. Chicago, 1961.
Logan, Rayford W. *The Negro in American Life and Thought: The Nadir, 1877-1901*. New York, 1954.
Loggins, Vernon. *The Negro Author*. New York, 1931.
McPherson, Edward. *The Political History of the United States During the Period of Reconstruction*. Washington, D.C., 1871.
McPherson, James M. *The Negro's Civil War*. New York, 1965.
————. *The Struggle for Equality: Abolitionists and the Negro in the Civil War and the Reconstruction*. Princeton, 1964.
Meier, August. *Negro Thought in America, 1880-1915*. Ann Arbor, 1963.
Myrdal, Gunnar. *An American Dilemma*. New York, 1962.
Olmsted, Frederick Law. *The Cotton Kingdom*. New York, 1861.
Parker, Jane Marsh. *Rochester, A Story Historical*. Rochester, 1864.
Penn, I. Garland. *The Afro-American Press and Its Editors*. Springfield, Mass., 1891.
Ricketson, Daniel. *The History of New Bedford*. New Bedford, 1858.
Scharf, J. Thomas. *History of Baltimore*. Baltimore, 1881.
Siebert, William. *The Underground Railroad*. New York, 1898.
Stampp, Kenneth M. *The Peculiar Institution: Slavery in the Antebellum South*. New York, 1956.
————. *The Era of Reconstruction, 1865-77*. New York, 1965.
Stanton, Elizabeth Cady; Anthony, Susan B.; and Gage, Matilda Joslyn. *History of Woman Suffrage*. 3 vols. Rochester, 1881.
Wade, Richard C. *Slavery in the Cities*. New York, 1967.
Weisberger, Bernard A. "The Dark and Bloody Ground of Reconstruction Historiography." *Journal of Southern History*. November 1959.
Wilson, Joseph T. *The Black Phalanx*. New York, 1888.
Woodson, Carter G., ed. *The Mind of the Negro as Reflected in Letters Written During the Crisis, 1800-1860*. Washington, D.C., 1926.
————. *The Negro in Our History*. Washington, D.C., 1922.
————. *Negro Orators and Their Orations*. Washington, D.C., 1925.
Woodward, C. Vann. *Reunion and Reaction*. Boston, 1966.
————. *The Strange Career of Jim Crow*. New York, 1957.
Wyman, Lillie Buffum Chace, and Crawford, Arthur. *Elizabeth Buffum Chace, Her Life and Its Environment*. Boston, 1914.

BIOGRAPHIES, AUTOBIOGRAPHIES, REMINISCENCES, AND LETTERS

Bartlett, Irving H. *Wendell Phillips: Brahmin Radical*. Boston, 1962.
Brogan, D. W. *Abraham Lincoln*. New York, 1963.
Brown, William Wells. *The Black Man: His Antecedents, His Genius and His Achievements*. Boston, 1863.
————. *Narrative of William W. Brown, A Fugitive Slave*. Boston, 1847.
Frothingham, Octavius Brooks. *Gerrit Smith*. New York, 1878.
Garrison, Wendell P. and Francis J. *William Lloyd Garrison, 1805-79*. 4 vols. Boston, 1885 and 1889.

Hutchinson, John Wallace. *Story of the Hutchinsons*. Boston, 1896.
May, Samuel J. *Some Recollections of Our Anti-Slavery Conflict*. Boston, 1869.
Rice, Allen Thorndike. *Reminiscences of A. Lincoln by Distinguished Men of His Time*. New York, 1888.
Rollin, Frank A. *Life and Public Services of Martin R. Delaney*. Boston, 1883.
Sanborn, Frank B., ed. *Life and Letters of John Brown*. Boston, 1891.
——————. *Recollections of Seventy Years*. 2 vols. Boston, 1909.
Sandburg, Carl. *Abraham Lincoln: The War Years*. 4 vols. New York, 1939.
Sears, Lorenzo. *Wendell Phillips: Orator and Agitator*. New York, 1909.
Still, William. *The Underground Railroad*. Philadelphia, 1872.
Terrell, Mary Church. *A Colored Woman in a White World*. Washington, 1940.
Thomas, John L. *The Liberator: William Lloyd Garrison*. Boston, 1963.
Villard, Oswald Garrison. *John Brown, 1800-1859*. Boston, 1910.
Ward, Samuel Ringgold. *Autobiography of a Fugitive Negro*. London, 1855.

index